Happy Cooking
Jenny Thomson

VEG FOR
VITALITY

How To Cook Simple
Vegetarian Recipes

BY JENNY THOMSON

Limits of Liability & Disclaimer Of Warranty

The author and publisher shall not be liable for your misuse of this material – this book is strictly for educational and information purposes only.

Warning and disclaimer

The purpose of this book is to educate and to entertain. The author and publisher do not guarantee that anyone following these suggestions, techniques, tips, ideas or strategies will achieve a particular result. The author/publisher shall have neither liability or responsibility to anyone with respect to any loss or damage caused, or alleged to be caused directly or indirectly by the information contained in this book.

Who is Jenny Thomson?

Jenny is a chef with over 30 years of cookery & 10 years of teaching experience. In 2011 she threw open the doors of her family home to share her skills & passion for fresh, seasonal produce.

Jenny has developed a range of cookery classes to help inspire you to improve your cookery skills and eat better. Boost your confidence, become more efficient & intuitive in the kitchen, whatever your culinary level.

She lives in Fife and in her spare time enjoys coastal rowing, walking, cycling and rock climbing.

Contents

Veg for Vitality

Introduction

Vegetables are superfoods!

They come in a variety of rainbow colours, flavours and textures. The stronger the colour, the more nutrients they contain. They are endlessly versatile, don't take much preparation, are quick to cook and don't have gristly bits!! We should be eating five or more portions per day.

There has a been a lot written about diet over the years – eat more of this, eat less of that, go vegan, don't eat carbs, count calories, have fasting days in the week….

The diet industry is big business, but it's confusing, can be misleading and expensive.

At the end of the day, in order to survive and be in optimum health, we need a range of proteins, carbohydrates and fats every day for our bodies to extract the nutrients, vitamins and minerals needed for energy, cell regeneration and immune strength.

The way to achieve this is, instead of counting calories (vegetables are a low calorie food), we should be looking at the amount of vitamins and minerals a food has.

Aubergines and carrots don't come with a food label and actually, food labels don't tell you what the levels of individual vitamins and mineral are, so if you can eat as unrefined foods as possible, everything in moderation, none in excess. You'll be pretty close to achieving optimum health.

What is refined food?

Refined food is any food not in its natural state, so flour, sugar, fruit juice…

You can improve on this by swapping what you eat, for example, eating wholemeal bread instead of white, using brown rice instead of white, eating a piece of fruit or a handful of nuts instead of juice, crisps or biscuits. Ditching fizzy drinks for water…

If you're not used to eating like this, it will be daunting, but start with one thing and work up. Over time you will see a difference to your skin, hair, nails, digestion, mood, weight and general health. It will become second nature to eat like this and doesn't mean you can't ever have a pizza or fish & chips again, just don't have them very often.

This book is a collection of my favourite vegetable dishes. They are dishes I make for my family on a regular basis, some I teach in my cookery classes.

There are stand-alone vegan and vegetarian dishes here, you can add a steak or fillet of fish if you feel the need. Most recipes are gluten and dairy free or can be easily made so just by swapping an ingredient or two. Enjoy this book, use it as inspiration to change your life and diet for the better.

Alliums

Onions, leeks, shallots, spring onions, chives and garlic all belong to the allium family.

We'll start with garlic here, known as **'The King of Herbs'** it has been used for medicinal purposes through the

centuries. Garlic's strong odour, due to the sulphurous compounds within it, not only adds flavour and depth to a dish, but helps to purify the body.

With immune-enhancing properties and antioxidant phytochemicals, it helps eliminate toxins, reduce blood pressure and blood cholesterol levels when used over time. It is used in respiratory infections such as chronic bronchitis, catarrh, recurrent colds and influenza.

The more garlic is crushed, the stronger the flavour and medicinal properties become. If you want power, use a lot and chop or crush it finely. For a subtle flavour, infuse a whole, peeled or unpeeled clove into whatever you're making, then either remove or mash the softened garlic into the sauce. To obtain the most medicinal properties, eat it raw, finely chopped and sprinkled over food, or blended into a salad dressing. Raw garlic becomes more pungent as it sits, so if you're not going to eat it straight away, use slightly less than stated in a recipe.

Onions, whether they are brown, yellow, red or white, green leeks, spring onions or chives, have very similar properties to garlic, but work in a more subtle way.

What to look for

Onions, garlic and shallots are grown over the summer, then dried to last over winter. Look for vegetables that are firm, without sprouts, soft patches or mould.

Leeks and spring onions are grown and harvested all year round. Spring onions will be tunnel grown or imported from abroad. You're looking for good green tops, that are not dull, wizened or browning.

Chives are a perennial, dying back over the winter and sprouting again in the spring. Over winter they will be imported or tunnel grown.

How to prepare them

Onions, remove any dirt and excess roots, peel off the papery skin and either slice, dice or cut the onion into wedges. If you're putting raw onion into salad, slice or dice it as thinly as possible as it can have a strong flavour.

Keeping the root on or washing your board, knife and hands regularly with cold running water will help if you're prone to 'onion tears'. Whatever you do, don't wipe your eyes with an oniony hand!

For leeks, keep the root intact, split them lengthways and run them under the cold tap from root to tip, removing any dirt with your fingers as you go.

How to cook & use them

Onions can be cooked whole, sliced, chopped, fried, boiled, baked or roasted. From a puree to an infusion, onions are one of the most versatile vegetables in terms of flavour. Sharp & punchy when eaten raw or sweet and mellow if slowly & gently cooked.

Leeks have a milder flavour to onions and are best sliced fairly thinly. If you're going to char grill or roast them whole, use young, thin specimens. Leeks are a superb addition to soups, sauces, pies and tarts.

Use them instead of onions at any point in time.

Spring onions & chives

These are both best sliced finely and used raw either sprinkled into salads or stirred into stir fries or casseroles at the last minute. Spring onions and chives are milder again than onions.

Leek Soufflé Tart

Serves 4 - 5

This is one of my favourite recipes, because it's a thicker mixture, if your pastry has a few cracks, it won't flow through!

Pastry

6oz/175g plain flour

3oz/85g butter

1 egg

Grind of black pepper

Filling

1 medium leek – finely sliced

¼ tsp. turmeric

1 tbsp. olive oil

1 tbsp. flour

2 eggs separated

1 tbsp. lemon

1 tbsp. parsley

1oz/30g grated parmesan cheese

100ml milk

50ml Greek yogurt, crème fraiche or double cream

1. Make the pastry either in a food processor or by hand: combine the flour and butter until the mixture is like crumbs, add the black pepper and egg and bring together to form a ball of dough. Wrap in cling film and allow to rest for 20 min in the fridge.

2. Set the oven to 200C/400F/gas6

3. Roll the pastry out thinly, line a 20cm flan ring or dish and bake blind in the oven for 15 min or until the edges of the pastry begin to turn golden.

4. Sweat the leeks in the olive oil until soft.

5. Add the turmeric and flour and cook for a minute.

6. Remove from the heat, add the milk and stir well to combine.

7. Return the pan to the heat and bring gently to the boil to make a sauce.

8. Remove the pan from the heat, allow to cool slightly and add the parmesan cheese, yogurt, parsley, lemon juice and salt and pepper.

9. Add the egg yolks and stir to combine.

10. Whip the egg whites to stiff peak and fold into the leek mixture.

11. Turn the oven down to 180C/350F/gas5 and bake tart for 20 – 30 minutes until set, puffed up and golden brown.

Hints, Tips and Variations

To make dairy free, swap the butter, yogurt & cheese for dairy free alternatives. Reheat in a microwave.

Instead of leeks, vary the filling with mushrooms, cooked red pepper, crab meat, smoked salmon…

Leek and Sweet corn Chowder

Serves about 6

A chowder is a thick, hearty meal in a bowl. Perfect for having in the fridge ready to eat when hunger strikes.

4 cobs sweet corn

500g floury potatoes, diced

1 large leek, cleaned and finely sliced

800ml chicken or vegetable stock

15g butter

½ tsp. mixed herbs

Small bunch of parsley

1. Cut the sweetcorn kernels off the cobs, heat the butter in a heavy based pan and fry the sweetcorn and leek for a few minutes to soften.
2. Add the diced potato, mixed herbs and the stock. Bring to the boil, reduce the heat to a simmer, put a lid on the pan and cook for 20mins.
3. Chop the parsley and add to the soup once finished. Check the seasoning and serve.

Hints, Tips and Adaptations

Gluten free, use oil instead of butter to make this dairy free, freezable, microwavable.

Use a couple of tins of sweetcorn if you don't want to use fresh

Use onion instead of leek

Onion Bhajis

Makes about 6

2 large onions

sea salt

1 tsp. coriander seed

1 tsp. cumin seed

½ mugful gram flour

about 6 tbsps. water

1. Slice the onions into approx. 5mm slices. Put into a colander or sieve and sprinkle with 1 tsp. salt. Allow to sit for 30min to release some of their liquid.
2. Grind the coriander and cumin seed in a mortar & pestle with ½ tsp salt and a good grinding of black pepper. Mix into the gram flour and add the water to make a thick batter.
3. Rinse the onions and squeeze as much moisture out of them as possible. Mix with the spiced batter
4. Heat about 1cm depth oil in a heavy based frying pan, once the oil is hot enough to start sizzling when a piece of onion is dropped into it, put small handfuls of onion batter into the oil. Cook on a medium heat for about 5 min before turning and frying for another 5 min.
5. Drain on kitchen paper & keep warm in a low oven until needed.

Spicy Green Sauce

Small bunch of mint, coriander and flat leaf parsley

1 small clove garlic

1 -2 green chillies to taste

Pinch of salt

Pinch of sugar

juice of ½ lime

1. Roughly chop the herbs, de seed & chop the chillies depending on how hot you would like your sauce.
2. Put everything into a blender or food processor and blitz to a smoothish wet paste – add a little water if necessary.

Provencal Onion Tart

Serves 2

200g puff pastry

500g onions

1 tbsp olive oil

1 small clove garlic, chopped

1 tsp chopped thyme

3 tsp chopped parsley

Pinch of sugar

½ tin anchovy fillets or roasted red pepper strips

Black olives

1. Set the oven to 200C/400F/Gas6

2. Roll the pastry out to approx. 15 x 25cm, neaten the edges with a knife and place on a baking sheet. Score a 1 cm border around the edge, make sure you cut into the corners and don't go all the way through the pastry.

3. Carefully score a criss-cross pattern over the middle of the pastry, lightly brush the edge with milk and bake in the oven until the pastry is risen and golden.

4. Thinly slice the onions, heat the olive oil in a heavy based pan and gently fry for about 20 mins., or until the onions are soft and beginning to colour.

5. Stir through the chopped garlic, thyme and parsley, add a pinch of sugar, stir well and remove from the heat.

6. Spread the onions over the cooked pastry base, slice each anchovy in half lengthways and arrange in a lattice pattern over the onions. Place a whole or half olive in the centre of each diamond shape.

7. Turn the oven down to 180C/350/Gas4 and bake the tart for another 15 mins to allow the flavours to mingle.

Brassicas

The Green Goddess of the vegetable world...

Brassicas are part of the mustard family and include broccoli, cauliflower, Brussels sprouts, cabbage, kale, kohlrabi, radishes, Chinese vegetables mizuna and bokchoi.

They are packed full of good health benefitting nutrients for heart health, cancer prevention, skin and eye health including antioxidant carotenoids, sulphur rich compounds, minerals potassium, iron and selenium, vitamin C & folic acid as well as a host of others.

What to look for

Broccoli, cauliflower & sprouts look for good tight heads without yellowing or brown patches.

Cabbages should have a tight heart and the outer leaves should again be crisp, although outer leaves can be removed before preparing.

If your broccoli or kale is a little bit soft around the edges, cut a slice off the end of the stalk and put it into water for a few hours. Like a flower it will firm up and become crisp again.

How to prepare it

The whole of the brassica can be eaten – stalk, leaves and flower heads, which makes it incredibly environmentally friendly, there shouldn't be any waste at all.

Floret broccoli and cauliflower, slice cabbage & kale either coarsely or finely depending on what you want to do with it. Cauliflower can also be cut into 'steaks' or kept whole for roasting.

How to cook it

Steaming, roasting or stir frying will retain the most amount of nutrients, the main thing is to avoid boiling them as almost all the nutrients will be lost in the process.

To avoid the 'boiled cabbage' sulphurous smell, cook brassicas lightly until just cooked, but still with a bite. They should still be bright green and crisp.

Removing the 'boiled cabbage' aroma

If you do end up over cooking your cabbage or broccoli, sit a bowl of white vinegar in a bowl in your kitchen overnight. This will help neutralise that over boiled aroma.

Baked Spiced Cauliflower

Serves 3 – 4

1 medium cauliflower

1 tsp ground coriander

1 tsp cumin seed

¼ tsp ground turmeric

½ tsp salt

½ tsp ground black pepper

3 tbsp oil

2cm piece root ginger, shredded

2 fresh tomatoes, chopped

100g sweet pepper, chopped

1. Set the oven to 190C/375F/Gas5
2. Cut the cauliflower into florets about 3cm size. Keep the stalk on the florets.
3. Put the pepper, tomatoes, ground coriander, turmeric, salt, pepper & oil into a blender and blitz to a paste. Stir through the cumin seed and shredded ginger.
4. Grease a small roasting tin with a little oil, put in the cauliflower and pour over the paste. Mix well and put into the oven for 30mins, turning half way through to give some dark, charred areas to the cauliflower. The paste will reduce and thicken. If it gets too thick, add a little water.
5. Serve with snipped chives and fragrant rice.

Brussels Sprouts with Chestnuts and Orange Herb Butter

Serves 8

30g butter - softened

zest of ½ orange

1 tbsp. chopped herbs – parsley, thyme

1 Kg fresh Brussels sprouts – prepared and ready to cook

200g cooked and peeled chestnuts – roughly chopped

1. Put the butter, orange zest and herbs in a bowl with a little salt and pepper and mash together until smooth. Tip onto a piece of cling film, roll into a sausage shape and chill.
2. Cook the sprouts – either boil or steam until tender. Refresh under cold water briefly
3. Once cooked, remove from the heat, melt ½ the butter in a heavy based frying pan, add the chestnuts and cook, stirring for 2 minutes, add the sprouts and heat through for another 2 minutes.
4. Tip into a serving dish and dot with the remaining butter if necessary before serving.

Chermoula Cauliflower Wedges with Kale & Mango Salad

Serves 4

There was a craze for cauliflower steaks, but you only get about 2 good slices from the middle of a cauliflower, so I've done wedges instead. A lovely supper for a warm spring day.

1 medium cauliflower

4 tbsps. chermoula paste (I used Belazu)

1 tbsp. oil

½ bag shredded kale

1 tbsp. olive oil

1 tsp. wine vinegar

¼ tsp. Dijon mustard

pinch dried mixed herbs

1 little gem lettuce, sliced

1 unripe mango

100g feta cheese, sliced into 8 pieces

1 small red onion, finely sliced

2 tbsps. red wine vinegar

1 tsp. sugar

1. Heat the oven to 220C/425F/Gas7.

2. Finely slice the red onion, mix with the red wine vinegar and sugar, set aside

3. Cut through the stem of the cauliflower to make 8 wedges. Mix the chermoula paste with the oil and rub over the wedges. Put into a baking tin in a single layer and put into the oven for 15 mins.

4. Mix the olive oil, wine vinegar, Dijon mustard & mixed herbs together to make a dressing. Pick over the kale, removing any large pieces of stalk. Drizzle over the dressing and massage it well into the kale for 30 seconds to help it soften.

5. Peel the mango and slice the flesh into matchsticks, mix into the kale.

6. Once the cauliflower has baked for 15 mins, remove from the oven, lay the feta slices over the wedges and return to the oven for 3 minutes.

7. To serve, mix the little gem lettuce into the kale and mango salad, divide onto 4 plates.

8. Remove the cauliflower from the oven and place 2 wedges on top of the salad on each plate.

9. Drain and discard the vinegar from the red onion, garnish each plate with a few onion slices.

Hints Tips & Adaptations

Gluten free, dairy free, vegetarian, re-heat in a microwave..

Use a bag of spicy salad leaves instead of kale, but just drizzle over the dressing at the last minute.

Use Wensleydale cheese instead of feta.

Chinese Style Kale with Poached Eggs on Toast

Serves 1

I harvested some of the kale growing in my garden for this. I used 6 black Tuscan kale leaves, but curly kale would work just as well.

A good handful of kale, sliced

1 tsp oil

1 spring onion, sliced

2 tsp tarragon, chopped

2 tsp soya sauce

2 medium eggs

Drizzle sweet chilli sauce

1 tsp sesame oil

1 slice sourdough bread

Pinch of paprika (optional)

1. Heat the oil in a small frying pan, add the kale, sliced spring onion and tarragon. Stir fry for a few moments until the kale begins to wilt. Add the soya sauce, simmer until the kale is tender and the vegetable juices have evaporated. Remove from the heat, stir through the sesame oil and keep warm.
2. Poach the eggs and toast the bread.
3. Finish the dish by covering the toast with the sesame kale mixture. Top with the poached eggs, drizzle with a little sweet chilli sauce and sprinkle over some paprika to finish the garnish.

Japanese Winter Red Cabbage Salad

Serves 4

I like red cabbage, but not always stewed. Finely shredding it into a salad is a delicious way of making the most of its' vibrant red colour.

Salad

¼ small red cabbage

½ gem lettuce

5cm piece daikon radish, or 4 pink radishes

1 small carrot

3 tbsps. coriander leaves

1 spring onion, finely sliced

1 tsp. sesame seeds

Soy & Ginger Dressing

2 tsps. grated root ginger

½ tbsp. malt vinegar

1 tbsp. sugar

½ tbsp. light soy

½ tbsp. dark soy

1 tbsp. tomato ketchup

1 tsp. lemon juice

1. Shred the cabbage and put into a salad bowl. Add shredded gem lettuce, grated daikon and carrot, finely sliced spring onion and coriander leaves. Toss well, sprinkle over the sesame seeds and drizzle over the dressing.

Hints, Tips and Variations

Dairy free, gluten free if using gluten free soya sauce & ketchup.

Use green or white cabbage instead of red.

Use other oriental vegetables instead of gem lettuce.

Kerelan Vegetables

Serves 1

This is a delicious way to jazz up cabbage or any vegetables, I like mine with poached eggs on top.

1 tbsp oil

1 tsp black mustard seed

½ tsp cumin seed

Pinch chilli flakes

1 tbsp root ginger, finely grated

¼ tsp ground turmeric

125g cabbage, sliced

1 med carrot, cut into 5mm dice

50g fresh or frozen grated coconut

1 green chilli, sliced (optional)

Salt & pepper

2 – 3 poached eggs (optional)

1. Heat the oil in a heavy based frying pan on a medium high heat. Add the mustard seed & when it starts to pop, add the cumin seed and chilli flakes.
2. Reduce the heat a little, add the ginger & turmeric.
3. Stir, then add the sliced cabbage and diced carrot.
4. Stir & mix everything well, add a splash of water to the pan, put a lid on the pan and leave to steam for 5mins.

5. Stir through the green chilli and coconut, taste for seasoning and serve.

Hints, Tips and Adaptations

Gluten free, dairy free, reheat in a microwave

Use different vegetables in season

If you can't get fresh coconut, use ½ the amount of desiccated

Poached Eggs on Toast with Stir Steamed Mustard Sprouts

Serves 1

I made this one night when I was home alone, a nice alternative to avocado. Sprouts, mustard and eggs go well together.

1 small onion, finely sliced

6 to 8 sprouts, finely sliced

1 tsp oil

5cm piece French bread or whatever you have.

2 eggs

5g butter

2 tsp chopped tarragon

½ tsp Dijon mustard

Splash white wine vinegar

Paprika to sprinkle (optional)

Salt & pepper

1. Bring a pan of water to the boil, add a splash of vinegar and poach the eggs for approx. 2 minutes each for a runny yolk.
2. Toast the bread
3. Heat the oil in a heavy based frying pan, add the sliced onion, fry for a few moments until softened, then add the sprouts. Stir fry again, add the mustard and a splash of water. Turn down the heat and put a lid on the

pan. Steam for 2 to 3 minutes, or until the sprouts are tender. Stir through ¾ of the tarragon, season with salt & pepper.

4. Tip the onions and sprouts onto the warm toast, top with the poached eggs, dot with butter and finish with a sprinkle of paprika.

Hints, Tips and Adaptations

Gluten free if you use gluten free toast, dairy free if you swap the butter for oil, vegetarian.

Replace the sprouts with any grated or finely sliced vegetables – carrot, parsnip, cabbage, red pepper, beans, baby corn, sugar snap peas, broccoli…

Swap the tarragon for parsley, dill or a mixture.

Quick Braised Red Cabbage

Serves 4

This is one of my favourite ways to cook red cabbage, it's not too stewed and has a light flavour.

½ red cabbage, cored & shredded

1 red onion, thinly sliced

1 clove garlic, thinly sliced

2 tbsp soft light brown sugar

2 tbsp balsamic vinegar

1 small star anise

½ tsp mixed spice

15g butter

1. Melt the butter in a medium pan, add the onion and cook gently to soften.
2. Add the garlic, sugar, vinegar, star anise and mixed spice. Mix everything well, then add the cabbage and stir everything together.
3. Put a tight-fitting lid on the pan and cook gently for 30 minutes, stirring from time to time. There should be enough moisture in the pan to stop it sticking, if you think the cabbage is getting a bit dry, add a splash of water.
4. Taste and add salt and pepper before serving.

Red Lentil Dal with Tandoori Cauliflower

Serves 4

I made this to warm us up on a cold night when sleet was battering the windows. It's quite a spicy dish, reduce or omit the chilli powder if you don't like hot spices

Red Lentil Dal

200g red split lentils

500ml water

¼ tsp. ground turmeric

¼ tsp. ground coriander

¼ tsp. garam masala

1 tbsp. oil

½ tsp. cumin seed

1 clove garlic

1 sm onion, chopped

½ tsp. chilli powder

2 tomatoes, chopped into 5mm pieces

½ tsp. salt

100g fresh spinach

Pepper to taste

1. Put the lentils, water, turmeric, coriander and garam masala into a heavy based pan. Bring to the boil, put a lid on the pan and simmer gently for 20mins.

2. In another pan, heat the oil, add the cumin, garlic and chopped onion. Fry gently to soften and add the chilli powder. Stir through and add the chopped tomatoes. Cook for 5 minutes and stir through the lentils once their 20mins is up. Remove from the heat and add the spinach. Stir through, allowing the heat of the dal to wilt and soften the leaves.

Tandoori Cauliflower

1 medium cauliflower

150ml Greek yogurt

2cm root ginger, finely grated

2 cloves garlic, finely grated

¼ tsp salt

¼ tsp ground turmeric

½ tsp chilli powder

½ tsp garam masala

¼ tsp ground coriander

1. Heat the oven to 220C/425F/Gas7
2. Steam the cauliflower for 5 mins to par cook.
3. Mix the yogurt with the ginger, garlic, salt and spices.
4. Tip the cauliflower into a roasting pan, drizzle over the yogurt mixture and toss well to coat.
5. Roast in the oven for 10 minutes to heat through and brown a little.
6. Serve the cauliflower with the dal spooned over the top.

Hints, Tips and Adaptations

Gluten free, microwavable

Try broccoli, carrots, squash, sweet potato, celeriac, swede, parsnips or aubergine instead of cauliflower.

The dal will freeze & is dairy free, try kale instead of spinach.

Spice Baked Cauliflower with Tomato Sauce

Serves 4

Cauliflower is incredibly versatile & I'm always thinking of new ways to cook it. This one is a winner!

1 large cauliflower

400g new potatoes

1. Boil the potatoes for 10mins, drain and allow to cool enough to handle. Then cut into bite size pieces if necessary.
2. Cut the cauliflower into large florets and steam for 3 minutes to par cook.

Spice Marinade

4 tbsps. olive oil

1 tsp. ground turmeric

3 tsps. ground cumin

1 tsp. ground cinnamon

1 tsp. salt

3 cloves garlic, roughly chopped

10g coriander leaves & stems, chopped

5g mint leaves, chopped

1. Heat the oven to 200C/400F/Gas6

2. In a mortar & pestle or spice grinder, grind the salt & garlic together until you have a smooth paste. Add the spices, stir well and mix in enough olive oil to make a paste.

3. Put the cauliflower and potatoes into a roasting tin, dot over the spice paste and use your hands to mix everything together well. Try and get some of the paste down into the cauliflower florets and a good covering over the potatoes. Spread out into a layer and put into the oven for 30 minutes.

Sauce

2 tins of chopped tomatoes

1 tbsp. oil

1 large onion, chopped

2 fat cloves garlic, skinned but left whole

1 tsp. turmeric

1 tsp. cumin seed

1 tsp. ground ginger

2 tsp. soft brown sugar

1. Heat the oil in a deep pan, add the onion and garlic and fry gently to soften and begin to colour the onion.
2. Add the spices, mix, then add the tinned tomatoes and brown sugar . Stir everything together and simmer without a lid for 20 minutes.
3. Puree with a hand blender or liquidiser, taste for seasoning and keep warm.
4. When the cauliflower and potatoes have cooked, remove from the oven. To serve, divide onto plates and spoon over some of the sauce.

Hints, Tips and Adaptations

Gluten free, dairy free, vegan/vegetarian

Re-heat in the microwave.

Try this with broccoli, but don't cook as long.

Use the sauce with chicken, pasta or fish.

Steamed Cabbage & Quinoa

Serves 4

Very quick and easy to make a nice accompaniment to any dish.

1 mug quinoa

1 mug water

1 tsp vegetable bouillon

1 medium onion, sliced

½ cabbage or spring greens, sliced

1 tbsp oil

1. Put the quinoa, water and vegetable stock powder into a small pan with a lid. Bring to the boil, turn down to a low simmer and cook for 10mins. Once time is up, allow to sit with the lid on the pan until needed.
2. Heat the oil in a large frying pan, add the onion and fry gently to soften and brown a little. Add the cabbage or spring greens, mix the with onions and add a splash of water. Put a lid on the frying pan and steam for 2 - 4 mins, just until the cabbage is tender but still bright green.
3. Tip the quinoa into the cabbage mixture. Mix everything well, adjust the seasoning and serve.

Hints, Tips and Adaptations

Gluten free, dairy free, reheat in a microwave
Use different vegetables depending on what you have, thinly slice broccoli, carrots, kale, etc would all work & give a different flavour.

Warm Soba Noodle Stir Through

Serves 4

This stir through is incredibly quick and easy to make. Steam the veg to keep as many of the nutrients as possible.

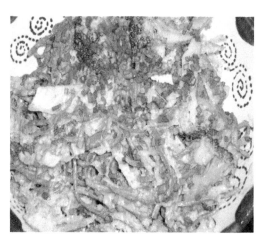

250g (3 portions) soba noodles

½ Savoy cabbage, shredded

Small head broccoli, floretted

Small bunch chives or 1 spring onion – finely sliced

Sauce

4 tbsps. almond or peanut butter

5 tbsps. water

2 tbsp. soy sauce

2 tbsps. grated root ginger

1 small clove garlic

1 tbsp. sesame oil

2 tbsps. rice vinegar

2 tsps. honey

1. Blend the sauce ingredients together using a stick blender

2. Use a steamer and put the broccoli florets in the bottom with the shredded cabbage on the top. Steam for about 5 mins, or until the broccoli is cooked but still has a crunch.

3. Cook the noodles at the same time a you are steaming the vegetables in a large pan of water until just cooked.

4. Toss the noodles, vegetables and sauce together either in one of the cooking pans if big enough or a large bowl. Divide into bowls and serve.

Hints, Tips & Alternatives

Dairy Free, vegetarian, vegan

Use vegetables in season, change the flavours with green beans, sugar snap peas, baby corn, carrots, asparagus, etc.

Cucurbits

This is the squash and gourd family, including pumpkin, butternut squash, courgette and cucumber.

Orange fleshed pumpkins are high in fibre, vitamin A, and generally pumpkins, squashes and courgettes have good amounts of potassium, phosphorus, silicon, iron, magnesium and calcium.

Pumpkin seeds contain good levels of zinc and other minerals. Medicinally, over the centuries, pumpkin and cucumber seeds have been used as a remedy for worms and tapeworms.

Cucumbers are mainly used in salads and also have a 'cooling' action on burns or irritated skin. If you have a curry that is on the hot and spicy side, eat cucumber raita with it to counteract the burning sensation in your mouth.

Laying a slice of cucumber over tired or inflamed eyes is a cooling and soothing remedy along with a cucumber paste for sunburnt skin.

What to look for

Cucumbers and courgettes should be firm, with a glossy skin. Anything soft or wizened is past it's best.

Pumpkins and squashes have a thicker skin and keep for longer, again check for soft areas that have been bruised and reject anything with mush or mould.

How to prepare & cook it

Cucumbers and courgettes can be used as they are, just wash, top and tail. Some people find cucumber skin hard to digest and this probably depends on the variety, with modern varieties being more digestible. The majority of nutrients are in the skin, so try not to peel them.

Cucumbers are usually eaten raw, slice or dice into salads or grate and mix with Greek yogurt for a delicious dip.

Courgettes have a firmer flesh and are great cut into sticks to have with a dip. They can also be stir fried, sauteed or roasted, whole if the courgette is bite size or sliced, chipped or diced if larger. Stuffed courgette flowers are a beautiful starter sometimes seen on restaurant menus.

Pumpkins and squashes have much tougher skin, which is harder to remove. If you roast wedges, the flesh can easily be scooped from the skin once the cooked.

A whole pumpkin, roasted with a casserole inside it makes a very impressive centre piece

Butternut Squash Hummus

Serves 4

I had a butternut squash in the fridge and wanted to make a change from soup for lunch. This is a winner!

600g butternut squash

2 tbsps. olive oil

½ tsp. ground cinnamon

Salt & pepper

2 tsps. harissa paste

40g tahini

70g Greek yogurt

1 clove garlic, smashed & peeled

50g feta cheese

Coriander leaves to garnish

1. Heat the oven to 200C/400F/Gas6
2. Peel, deseed and dice the squash into approx. 2cm pieces. Put into a roasting tin, sprinkle over the ground cinnamon, season with salt & pepper. Drizzle with olive oil and toss everything together well. Put into the oven and roast for 30mins.
3. Remove from the oven and tip the roasted squash into a food processor, add the harissa paste, tahini, yogurt and garlic. Pulse until you have a coarse puree. Taste and adjust the seasoning if necessary.

4. Tip onto a serving plate, swirl with the back of a spoon, crumble over the feta cheese & finish with a few coriander leaves. Serve with flat bread, vegetable sticks or savoury biscuits.

Hints, Tips and Adaptations

Gluten free, dairy free if you miss out the cheese & use dairy free yogurt, freezes.

Serve with vegetable sticks, crackers or crusty bread.

Sprinkle some toasted flaked almonds or seeds to the top.

Butternut Squashetti with Chickpeas & Pesto

Serves 1

140g piece of butternut squash, peeled

2 spring onions

1 small can chickpeas, drained

2 tsps. green pesto

1 tbsp. pumpkin seeds

1 tbsp. Greek yogurt

1 small clove garlic

Glug of olive oil

Salt & pepper to taste

Parsley to garnish

1. Toast the pumpkin seeds in a dry pan.
2. Spiralise, shred or coarsely grate the squash.
3. Thinly slice the spring onion, finely slice the garlic, roughly mash the chickpeas.
4. Heat the oil in a heavy based frying pan, add the chickpeas & garlic, fry for a couple of minutes, then add the spring onions. Fry for a few moments and add the squash.
5. Stir to heat through, then add the pesto & ½ the yogurt.
6. Stir everything together to heat through, taste, adjust seasoning & sprinkle over most of the pumpkin seeds.

7. Tip into a bowl, top with the remaining yogurt & pumpkin seeds to serve.

Courgette & Herb Pie

Serves 2

1 courgette – about 125g

Approx. 125g frozen leaf spinach

1 small onion

1 spring onion

3 to 4 sheets filo pastry

½ pack feta cheese (100g)

1 egg

1 tbsp. Greek yogurt

4 tbsps. chopped mixed fresh herbs – parsley, dill, mint, tarragon, coriander

Olive or rapeseed oil for brushing

sesame seeds for scattering

Equipment – 2 x 10cm pie tins or equivalent

1. Grate the courgette, sprinkle with salt and allow to sit in a colander for 20 min to drain some of the excess juice, then rinse and squeeze out as much moisture as possible.
2. Fry the onion in a little olive oil until soft, add the courgette and fry gently for another 5 min. Remove from the heat.
3. Preheat the oven to 200C/400F/gas6.
4. Unwrap the filo pastry, cut 3 sheets in half widthways, re-wrap the remaining sheets well and store in the fridge for future use.
5. Brush the inside of the tins with a little oil, then the top sheet of pastry and drape over an 10cm pie tin or equivalent. Repeat with the remaining

sheets angling the sheets slightly, so that you end up with 2 pie tins with 3 sheets of oiled filo pastry draped over them.

6. Beat the egg and yogurt together, add the spring onion, herbs, crumble in the feta cheese and season with pepper.

7. Tip into the onion and courgette mixture, mix well and pour into the lined tins.

8. Crinkle over the edges of the filo pastry up over the pie to cover the top. If the pastry doesn't meet in the middle, use an extra sheet to cover the gaps. Dot the crinkled pastry with more oil and sprinkle with sesame seeds.

9. Bake for about 30 min

10. Allow to cool for about 30 min before eating.

Cucumber and Dill Pickle

Makes 4 x 225g jars

This is a nice, mild pickle. Good with cold meat or cheese. It's important not to slice the cucumber too thin here. Thicker slices keep their shape and crunch for longer.

1kg cucumbers

3 small onions

2 tbsps. dill

250g granulated sugar

1 tbsp salt

200ml cider vinegar

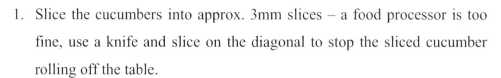

1. Slice the cucumbers into approx. 3mm slices – a food processor is too fine, use a knife and slice on the diagonal to stop the sliced cucumber rolling off the table.
2. Slice the onion finely
3. Mix the cucumber, onion and dill together.
4. Mix the sugar, salt and vinegar together, pour over the vegetables and allow to sit for 3 hours or overnight.
5. Pack into sterilised jars, cap. Store in the fridge and use within 2 weeks.

Cucumber & Mint Tzatziki

Serves 4 – 5

A delicious Greek dip.

½ cucumber

1 tbsp shredded mint

1 small clove garlic, crushed

100g Greek yogurt

Salt & pepper

1. Coarsely grate the cucumber, sprinkle with salt & allow the juices to drain for 20 mins. Rinse under cold water and squeeze as dry as possible.
2. Mix the cucumber, garlic, yogurt and mint together, season with salt & pepper, pile into a bowl to serve.

Cucumber Raita

Serves 8

½ cucumber

250ml Greek yogurt

½ tsp. cumin seed

¼ tsp. sugar

Salt & pepper to taste

1. Coarsely grate the cucumber into a colander, squeeze out as much moisture as possible with your hands.

2. Toast the cumin seeds in a dry pan for a few seconds, then mix with the yogurt, cucumber and sugar. Season with salt & pepper to taste.

Pumpkin Biryani

Serves 3 as a main course or 4 as a side

1 pumpkin - 1 to 1.5K in weight

2 small onions - sliced

2 cloves garlic - chopped

Thumb sized piece of root ginger - grated

1 red chilli (optional) - finely sliced

1/2 mug uncooked rice

1 tsp. each ground coriander & cumin

1/2 tsp. each ground cinnamon, nutmeg & turmeric

small handful each currants, flaked almonds & pistachio nuts

1. Set the oven to 200C/400F/Gas 6.
2. Cut the top off the pumpkin & scrape out the seeds.
3. Put the pumpkin into a roasting tray and roast for an hour, then remove from the oven, allow to cool a little & scrape out the flesh with a spoon. If the flesh is in big chunks, chop it up a bit.
4. Cook the rice.
5. Toast the almonds & pistachio nuts in a dry frying pan until golden.
6. Fry the sliced onion until starting to soften, add the ginger, garlic & chilli (if using). Add the ground spices, fry for a moment or two, and then add the pumpkin flesh, season with salt & pepper.
7. Layer the rice, nuts, currants & spicy pumpkin back into the pumpkin shell, place the lid of the pumpkin back on. Reduce the oven heat to

180C/350F/Gas4, pour about 2cm boiling water into the roasting tin with the pumpkin and cook for 45min before serving.

Spicy Squash Soup

Serves 3-4

1 small butternut squash peeled and deseeded

1 tbsp. oil

1 dried chilli, stalk and seeds removed or ¼ tsp. lazy chilli

some thyme sprigs

½ tbsp. cumin seed

1tsp coriander seed

1 onions chopped

1 garlic clove

Vegetable stock to cover

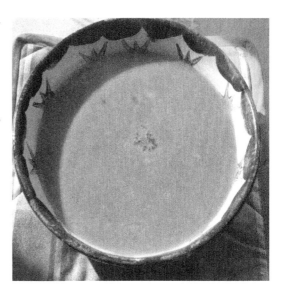

1. Cut the squash into large chunks and fry in the oil with the onions and garlic.
2. Dry fry the cumin and coriander seed in a small frying pan for a few moments and then grind in a mortar and pestle.
3. Add the stock to just cover the squash and onion.
4. Add the spices and chilli to the pot.
5. Simmer for 15 to 20 min, or until the squash is tender.
6. Liquidise and check for seasoning

Stuffed Butternut Squash

A delicious way to eat squash – this dish can be made in advance and re-heated. Use as a vegetarian main dish or accompaniment

1 butternut squash (800g)

40g feta cheese

¼ tsp dried mixed herbs

Pinch of chilli flakes

1/8th teaspoon ground cinnamon

¼ preserved lemon (10g)

4 – 5 sundried tomato pieces in oil (40g)

½ tsp ground coriander

1 clove garlic – thinly sliced

Black pepper

1. Heat the oven to 190C/375F/Gas5.
2. Cut the bulbous end off the squash and scoop out the seeds. Cut another slice about 5mm thick to use as a lid. Reserve the remainder of the squash for another dish.
3. Chop the sundried tomatoes & preserved lemon, crumble the feta cheese.
4. Mix everything together, pack into the squash cavity and top with the reserved slice. Rub the outside of the squash with a little of the sundried tomato oil and sprinkle with pepper.
5. Roast for 45min, allow to cool for 10 min before serving.

Stuffed Courgettes

1 courgette (200g)

1 spring onion – finely sliced

25g flaked almonds

1 tbsp breadcrumbs

1 tbsp finely grated Parmesan cheese

1 tbsp chopped herbs

1 tsp lemon rind

1 tsp olive oil

1. Set the oven to 220C/425F/Gas7
2. Toast the flaked almonds in a dry pan until golden and aromatic, mix with the Parmesan cheese, breadcrumbs, chopped herbs, lemon rind and olive oil.
3. While the hazelnuts are toasting, cut the courgette in half, length ways and scoop out the middle of each half with a tea spoon. Place in an ovenproof dish and roast in the oven for 10min.
4. In a small pan, on a high heat, fry the scooped-out courgette centres with a little oil brown and reduce the water content. Add the spring onion, mix with the courgette and remove from the heat. Season well with salt and pepper.
5. Once the courgettes have had their 10min, remove from the oven, divide the spring onion mixture between the two halves and top with the almond crumbs.
6. Return to the oven and bake for a further 10min.

Vegetable Goulash

Serves 3 – 4

We try to do 'meat free Monday'. After a busy weekend and limited supplies in the fridge, I made this. Thank goodness for a good store cupboard!

1 tbsp oil

1 onion, thinly sliced

2 courgettes, sliced

2 carrots, diced

¼ red cabbage, shredded

1 tin chopped tomatoes

1 tsp caraway seeds

1 tbsp paprika

½ tsp thyme

¼ tsp grated nutmeg

1 tsp vegetable bouillon

150ml Greek yogurt

1. Heat the oil in a heavy based pan, add the onion and carrot, sauté gently until the onion is soft.
2. Add the caraway seed & paprika. Stir well to combine and add the sliced courgette and cabbage. Stir again and add the chopped tomatoes, about ¼ tin of water, vegetable bouillon, thyme, nutmeg, season with salt & pepper.
3. Put a lid on the pan and simmer gently for 20 mins.

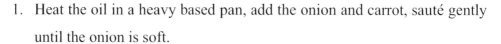

4. Stir through the yogurt and check the seasoning. Serve with rice or potatoes.

Hints, Tips and Adaptations

Gluten free, dairy free if you use plant based yogurt or coconut milk.

Use white cabbage if you don't have red.

Reheat in a microwave

Use whole milk Greek yogurt, low fat will split. You could also use crème fraiche or sour cream.

Fabulous Fennel & Celery

Ancient plants used as a herb, vegetable and seed.

The herb fennel is an ancient plant used for its herb, vegetable and seed. It's part of the carrot family (Apiaceae) along with carrots, celery, parsley, parsnip, caraway, chervil, coriander, dill, cumin & lovage.

Herb fennel originated in the Mediterranean, but is easy to grow in most soils and makes a good tall plant for the back of a border. The stalks can be dried and used for aromatic fuel on a barbecue, the fronds for salads, stuffing and stocks. The seeds for marinades, rubs, sprinkling onto bread or baking into biscuits.

Celery is one of those vegetables to always have in your fridge for adding flavour to soups, stews. It's also very low in calories, but packed with nutrients and has similar medicinal properties to fennel. Fennel and celery can be interchanged and swapped in most recipes, with similar results.

Fennel has a mild aniseed flavour and medicinally, along with celery is an excellent stomach and intestinal remedy, relieving flatulence, colic, soothing and stimulating digestion.

Fennel tea will increase the flow of milk in nursing mothers.

Florence fennel, bulb fennel and celery have edible stems. They have a crunchy texture with a juicy aniseed flavour and can be used thinly sliced in salad, simmered in soups, roasted, barbecued, steamed or braised.

Both fennel and celery are high in fiber, low in calories and packed with nutrients, particularly vitamin C, calcium, magnesium, potassium and phosphorus. They are calming on the digestive system, reducing indigestion, flatulence and constipation, help regulate blood pressure, menstruation, rheumatic and respiratory problems.

What To Do With Fennel & Celery

Pull the outer leaves off as they can be a bit tough. The inner bulb or heart is the best bit, tender and juicy for salads, steamed, roasted or braised as a vegetable or sliced up in casserole. Use the whole thing, stems and leaves.

The green stalks can be used to flavour stocks and soups. The feathery fronds or leaves can be used as a herb in salads and soups.

Braised Fennel

Serves 4

Slow cooking fennel makes it a delicious accompaniment to meat, poultry or fish. This is a traditional French way of cooking fennel.

2 bulbs of fennel, about 400g

4 cloves of garlic with the skin on

150ml white wine

2 tbsp oil

Salt & pepper

1. Cut the fennel bulbs into quarters or halves if small.
2. Heat a heavy based pan on a medium heat, add the oil and fry the fennel cut side down for about 5 min, each side to colour a little.
3. Add the garlic and white wine, it will bubble in the hot pan.
4. Turn the heat down, put a lid on the pan and simmer gently for 40mins or until tender.
5. Once cooked, remove the fennel from the pan & keep warm, remove the garlic cloves from their skins & mash into the pan juices. Boil to a syrupy consistency, then pour over the fennel. Finish with a scattering of fennel fronds.

Citrus Fennel Salad

Serves 4

A refreshing crisp salad ideal with roast lamb or duck, also good with oily fish like salmon, mackerel or herring.

1 red grapefruit

2 oranges

2 kiwi fruit

1 bulb fennel approx. 200 – 300g

Black pepper

Olive oil

1 heaped tbsp. shredded mint

1. With a knife, peel the grapefruit & oranges, then cut out the segments so that you have no pith or skin left on the fruit. Squeeze the juice from the core that is left and reserve.
2. Rub the kiwi fruit in a towel to remove some of the fuzz from the skin. Top & tail, then cut in half length wise and slice into approx. 5mm slices.
3. Finely slice the fennel, then toss with the kiwi, mint and citrus juices.
4. Spread over a platter or individual plates, arrange the citrus segments, drizzle with a little olive oil and a grind of black pepper.

Roast Fennel & Aubergine Salad

Serves 4

This salad can be either eaten warm or cold, the sharpness of the feta cheese complements the aniseed flavours of the fennel and creamy texture of the aubergine.

1 medium aubergine about 300g

1 large bulb fennel about 300g

2 tbsps. olive oil

1 tsp. cumin seed

200g pack feta cheese

Zest & juice of 1 lemon

25g chopped parsley

1. Heat the oven to 200C/400F/Gas6
2. Cut the aubergine into approx. 1.5cm chunks
3. Trim the fennel & cut into 8 wedges, with the root intact to keep the layers attached.
4. Put the aubergine and fennel into a roasting tin, drizzle over the oil, season with a pepper, a little salt & the cumin seed. Roast for 30 – 40 mins, until the vegetables have charred a little round the edges and the fennel is soft.
5. Cut or crumble the feta cheese into pieces, put into a bowl, mix with the lemon zest, juice and parsley.

When the aubergine and fennel are cooked, remove from the oven & mix everything together while the vegetables are still hot. Allow to cool and serve warm or at room temperature.

Roast Fennel with Red Peppers & Chickpeas

Serves 4

This dish can be a vegetarian main course or a salad. It has Middle Eastern flavours and can be spiced up or down to suit.

2 bulbs of fennel, about 400g

2 cloves garlic, skin on

12 cherry tomatoes

2 tbsps. oil

1 x 400g tin of chickpeas, drained & rinsed

2 roasted red peppers from a jar, drained & rinsed

25g fresh coriander

Dressing

1 ½ tsp. harissa paste

¼ preserved lemon rind, rinsed & chopped finely

3 tbsps. good olive oil

2 tbsps. lemon juice

1. Heat the oven to 200C/400F/Gas6
2. Cut the fennel into quarters, reserving any feathery tops. Put into a roasting tin, drizzle with oil, salt & pepper and roast for 20mins.

3. When the time is up, pierce the skin of the tomatoes and add them to one side of the roasting tin. Roast for another 20mins, then remove from the tin.

4. Cut the red peppers into strips, about 1cm thick, add them to the roasting tin once you have removed the tomatoes. Roast for 10mins, then add the chickpeas, stirring everything together & put back into the oven for a final 10mins.

5. Make the dressing – mash the roast tomatoes and mix with the harissa paste, preserved lemon rind, olive oil and lemon juice.

6. Roughly chop the coriander.

7. Once the roasting time is up, remove the roasting tin from the oven, drizzle the dressing over the fennel & chickpea mixture and mix well. Stir through the coriander and garnish with any reserved fennel tops.

Warm Salad of Poached Eggs with Fennel, Orange & Feta Cheese

Serves 2

Warm salads are lovely at this time of year. Fennel is just coming into season and goes well with orange and eggs. This dish is light, healthy, but still substantial enough to leave you satisfied.

1 bulb fennel

60g feta cheese

½ tsp. fennel seed

20g pine nuts

Zest of ½ orange

Juice of 1 orange

10g butter

1 tbsp. olive oil

100g white wine

2 handfuls of salad leaves

4 eggs

1. Crush the fennel seed a little, then put into a dry frying pan with the pine nuts and toast gently until the pine nuts are golden. Remove from the pan and set aside.
2. Cut the fennel into 8 to 12 wedges depending on its size. Reserve any fronds.

3. Heat the butter and oil in the frying pan and fry the wedges on a medium high heat for a few minutes each side to colour and soften the fennel.

4. Scatter the orange zest into the pan, add the white wine and bubble to reduce. Add the orange juice and continue to cook until there are about 3 teaspoons of liquid left. Remove the pan from the heat.

5. Poach the eggs.

6. Arrange the salad leaves on two plates or bowls, divide the fennel between them, arranging it on top of the leaves. Crumble over the feta cheese, then sprinkle over the pine nuts and fennel seeds.

7. Drain the eggs well, place on top of the salad, drizzle over the pan juices and finish with the reserved fennel fronds.

Warm Soba Noodle Bowl

Serves 1

Soba noodles are made with percentage of buckwheat flour, so are more delicate than Chinese, Udon or Ramen noodles.

About 150g mixed vegetables e.g.: carrot, celery, cabbage, Chinese leaves, pak choi, spring onion, frozen peas or beans, pepper, radish, spinach etc.

Pinch of chilli flakes (optional)

1 portion soba noodles

1 tsp. oil

Parsley or coriander to finish

Dressing

1 tbsp. soy sauce

1 tsp. tomato ketchup

2 tsps. rice or wine vinegar

½ tsp. finely grated root ginger

1 small clove garlic, grated

1 tsp. sesame oil

1. Make the sauce and set aside
2. Depending on what vegetables you are using, finely slice peppers, cabbage, spring onion, pak choi, celery. Coarsely grate any carrot, radish etc.

3. Cook the noodles in plenty boiling water, they only take a few minutes. Drain and rinse under running water.

4. Heat a small frying pan to hot, add the oil and when it starts to smoke, add all the vegetables plus the chilli flakes and stir fry for a few minutes to wilt and heat them through. Remove from the heat.

5. Mix with the dressing and warm noodles, pile into a bowl and eat!

Hints, Tips & Alternatives

Dairy free.

Use whatever veg is in the fridge

Legumes

The legume family include all peas and beans, fresh or dried. They are edible seeds that grow in pods after the plant has flowered.

They are a very good source of inexpensive protein and also contain complex carbohydrates with good fibre qualities, low calories and low fat content.

Dried beans contain varying levels of B vitamins, thiamine, niacin and pantothenic acid. There is a good level of iron in most dried beans as well as calcium, potassium and phosphorus.

It's important to eat a wide variety of beans, especially if you're vegetarian as the proteins within them are not as complete as animal protein. In order to obtain all the essential amino acids for a healthy body, we need to mix beans with other vegetable proteins and grains.

Dried beans also have the dubious reputation of being 'windy'. This is caused by fermenting oligosaccharides from the beans fermenting in the large intestine. These starch type molecules are found mainly in the bean skins, so soaking beans overnight, then discarding and rinsing beans before cooking will help to remove some of these fermenting properties. Adding a little bicarbonate of soda to the bean cooking water also helps to reduce the 'windy' properties of beans.

Fresh peas and beans contain more vitamin A, B vitamins and vitamin C than dried and also have good levels of minerals iron, potassium, calcium and magnesium.

Green beans in all their forms and peas whether, sugar snap or podded are best steamed or boiled very briefly to retain as much of their nutrients as possible.

Sprouts

Almost all beans, grains and seeds so long as they are fresh and in their most natural, dried form, can be sprouted.

When a seed is sprouted, the nutrients within the seed or bean are used to produce the beginnings of a new plant. Protein levels increase along with fibre and vitamin levels, they are a great addition to salads or sprinkled over the top of stir fries.

Black Bean Chilli

Serves 4

This has quite a kick, use less chilli if you like it milder.

1 tin black beans or ½ mugful dried beans, soaked and cooked, cooking liquid reserved.

1 tbsp. oil

1 red onion

1 red pepper

1 beetroot, tennis ball sized

1 red chilli (optional)

1 clove garlic

1 tin chopped tomatoes

2 tsps. paprika

1 tsp. smoked paprika

1 tsp. chilli flakes (optional)

2 tbsps. dark soy sauce

25g 70% dark chocolate, broken into pieces

1. Chop the onion, pepper, beetroot, chilli and garlic, fry in a large pan gently to soften.
2. Add the paprika, smoked paprika and chilli flakes, stir and add the beans and tin of tomatoes.
3. Bring to a simmer, if the mixture is a bit dry, add some of the reserved bean cooking liquid or water to come just under the top of the chilli.

Cook with the lid on for 30 mins, then with the lid off for 15 mins to reduce the sauce a little.

4. Stir through the soy sauce and dark chocolate, season with salt and pepper.

5. Serve with rice and a spoonful of tomato and avocado salsa.

Hints, Tips and Adaptations

Dairy free, gluten free, vegetarian, microwavable

Use red kidney beans or adzuki beans instead of black beans.

For the salsa, chop up avocado & tomato, stir in a squeeze of lime & some herbs.

Edamame Rice

Serves 4

Edamame beans are delicious, bright green and crispy, they make a change from frozen peas or broad beans. Find them in the freezer isle of your supermarket. This recipe uses Japanese flavours.

¾ mug basmati rice

¾ mug water

200g edamame beans

2 tbsps. sushi ginger, chopped

4 sprigs of basil, chopped

1 spring onion, thinly sliced

2 tbsps. rice wine vinegar (or wine vinegar)

1 tbsp. sugar

½ tsp. salt

½ tsp. soy sauce

1. Wash the rice to remove excess starch, put into a heavy based pan with the water, bring to the boil, put a lid on the pan and simmer very gently for 10 mins. Remove from the heat and allow to sit.
2. Mix the vinegar, sugar, salt & soy sauce together.
3. Cook the edamame beans by bringing to the boil, then draining.
4. Stir everything together and serve.

Hints, Tips and Adaptations

Dairy free, gluten free if using gluten free soya sauce, vegetarian, suitable for vegans.
Use frozen peas, broad beans or sweetcorn if you don't have edamame beans.
Use sushi rice if you'd like a sticky rice, follow the instructions on the packet for cooking.

Green Bean Salad with Feta Cheese

Serves 1

I like green beans and I like a warm salad; this is a winner!

1 handful of green beans, topped

1 handful of romaine or gem lettuce

6 cherry tomatoes, halved

8 black olives

2cm slice feta cheese

1 spring onion, thinly sliced

Squeeze of lemon juice

Pinch of salt & grind of black pepper

1. Steam the beans for a few minutes until tender, but still with a slight crunch. Remove from the heat and refresh under cold water. Allow to drain, then cut in half.
2. Slice the lettuce and toss with the beans, halved cherry tomatoes & olives.
3. Sprinkle over the sliced spring onion and crumble over the feta cheese. Sprinkle over a pinch of salt, a grind of black pepper and drizzle with a squeeze of lemon juice to serve.

Hints, Tips and Adaptations

Gluten free, for dairy free, swap the cheese for croutons, boiled potatoes, beans/chickpeas etc

I didn't add oil as my olives had oil on them. If you're olives are brined, drizzle a little olive oil.

Swap the beans for sugar snap or mange tout peas.

Green Lentil Salad with Thai Dressing

Serves 2 - 3

These lentils are spicy and refreshing with a Thai Dressing. Eat them warm from the pot or cold the next day.

150g green lentils

200ml water

2 handfuls gem or romaine lettuce

1 handful rocket

1 roasted red pepper, either from a jar or roasted from fresh

140g frozen edamame beans

3 spring onions, finely sliced

1 red or green chilli (optional or to taste)

1 small clove garlic, finely chopped

1 tbsp. coriander, roughly chopped

2 tbsps. lime juice

2 tbsps. fish sauce

2 tsp. soft brown sugar

1. Put the lentils and water into a pan, bring to the boil, put a lid on the pan and simmer on a low heat for 20 mins.
2. If using a fresh red pepper, grill on a high heat until the skin is blistered & blackened on all sides. Remove to a bowl, cover with a lid or cling

film and allow to cool. Once cool, scrape away the skin, remove the seeds & pith and chop into pieces. If using a red pepper from a jar, just drain and chop into pieces.

3. Bring the edamame beans to the boil in a small pan, remove from the heat and drain. Put hot into a bowl and mix through the pepper, finely sliced spring onions, chopped garlic, chilli if using and coriander.

4. Mix the lime juice, fish sauce and brown sugar together to make a dressing.

5. When the lentils are ready, while still hot, tip them into the bowl with the peppers, beans etc. Pour over the dressing and mix well.

6. To serve, divide the salad leaves between 2 or 3 plates and spoon over the lentils.

Hints, Tips and Adaptations

Gluten free, dairy free, for vegetarians, use soya sauce or liquid aminos instead of fish sauce.

Use black lentils instead of green. Don't be tempted to use the bigger brown lentils, they will be too 'meally'.

Green Lentils & Rice with Roasted Roots & Tomato Relish

Serves 6 to 8

I made this for someone who was dairy intolerant, it's based on Middle Eastern Mejadra, a lentil & rice dish usually served with a yogurt & cucumber sauce. The roasted roots & tomato relish replace the moisture from the traditional yogurt dressing.

Roasted Roots

Approx 200g each carrots, beetroot and butternut squash, cut into 1cm pieces. Drizzle with oil, toss with salt & pepper and roast at 200C for 20mins. Remove from the oven and allow to cool.

Lentils and Rice

3 medium onions

4 tbsp flour

1 mug small green lentils

¾ mug basmati rice

2 tsp cumin seed

3 tsp coriander seed

2 tbsp olive oil

½ tsp turmeric

1 tsp allspice

1 tsp ground cinnamon

350ml water

Oil for frying

Salt & pepper

Tomato Relish

2 large tomatoes, finely diced

¼ red onion, finely chopped

¼ red pepper, finely diced

Large clove of garlic, crushed

2 tsp balsamic vinegar

1tsp soft brown sugar

½ tsp ground allspice

3 tbsp olive oil

2 tsp chopped mint leaves

1. Finely slice the onions, toss with flour, salt & pepper.
2. Heat about 1 cm oil in a large frying pan. When the oil is hot fry the onions in 3 to 4 batches until brown and crisp. Drain on kitchen paper and set aside.
3. Put the lentils in a pan, cover with plenty water. Bring to the boil and simmer for 15 mins then drain and set aside. They should be par cooked and still have a bit of bite.

4. Make the relish: put everything into a bowl and stir together

5. Heat a heavy based pan on a medium high heat. Add the cumin and coriander seeds, fry for a few moments to warm through and toast. Add the rice with to the pan with 2 tablespoons olive oil, turmeric, allspice and cinnamon. Stir to toast and coat the rice with the oil and spices. Add the lentils and water. Bring to the boil, put a lid on the pan and simmer for 15mins.

6. Stir through the roasted vegetables and half the crispy onions.

7. Serve piled onto plates, with the relish spooned around the edge, topped with the remaining crispy onions.

Red Dragon Pie

Serves 6 – 8

This dish will suit vegetarians, vegans and carnivores alike, it's a one stop meal that only needs a bit of salad to spin it out even further.

½ mug dry adzuki beans or 1 tin

650g mixed red, yellow and orange vegetables. I used squash, beetroot, red onion, red pepper and sweet potato

1 clove garlic

½ tsp. chilli powder

1 tbsp. paprika

½ tsp. ground turmeric

1 tin chopped tomatoes

¾ tsp. salt

1 tbsp. oil

700g (8small) floury potatoes with skin on

2 tbsps. oil

Salt & pepper

1. If using dry beans, soak overnight, then cook in unsalted water for around 30mins until tender, drain
2. Cut the vegetables into 5mm dice, put into a heavy based pan with 1 tablespoon oil and fry on a medium heat until starting to soften.

3. Add the garlic, turmeric, chilli powder and paprika. Stir well and add the tomatoes plus ½ tin of water. Simmer for 10 mins, then add the cooked beans, stir everything well and cook for a further 10 mins.

4. Season with salt & pepper to taste.

5. Boil the potatoes in their skins. Once cooked, drain and allow to steam dry and cool enough to handle.

6. Slice the potatoes into about 3 slices each, put into a bowl, drizzle over 2 tbsp oil and season with salt & pepper. Toss gently to combine the oil and seasoning with the potato slices.

7. Pre-heat the oven to 200C/400F/Gas6

8. Tip the bean mixture into a casserole dish, top with the potato, overlapping the slices, then put into the oven and bake for 30 to 40 mins or until the contents of the casserole are hot and bubbling and the potatoes have crisped.

9. Serve as it is or with a side salad.

Hints, Tips & Alternatives

Dairy free, gluten free, freezable, microwavable

Change the flavours by using different beans – chickpeas, kidney beans, mung beans etc.

Add some herbs – thyme, rosemary, sage or parsley.

Spice it up with chilli, curry powder or paste.

Use mash instead of sliced potatoes

Stir Fried Peas and Beans

Serves 4

This is a very quick vegetable dish to jazz up frozen peas. Edamame beans are bright green and crunchy, they go well with tender peas.

125g frozen peas

125g frozen edamame beans

1 Romaine lettuce heart, or 2 little gem lettuces, sliced into approx. 5mm slices

1 tbsp. olive oil

1 small onion, thinly sliced

Juice of ½ lemon

Handful chopped mint

Salt & pepper

1. Cook the peas and beans into a small pan with 1cm water. Bring to the boil, remove from the heat and drain. Set aside to keep warm while you finish the recipe.
2. Heat the oil in a large frying pan, add the sliced onion and fry gently to soften, but not colour.
3. Turn up the heat a little, add the shredded lettuce, stir and when it begins to wilt, add the peas and beans. Squeeze over the lemon juice, season with salt & pepper and toss through the mint.
4. Serve immediately in a warm bowl.

Hints, Tips and Adaptations

Gluten & dairy free, vegetarian.

Finely shredded cabbage, spring greens, pak choi, bok choi or Chinese leaves would also work instead of lettuce.

Thai Red Lentil Soup

Serves about 6

A delicious fresh but warming soup on a dull day!

1 onion, chopped

2 medium carrots, chopped

2 celery sticks, chopped

1 tbsp. oil

2 lemon grass stalks, bashed & sliced

2 heaped tablespoons red curry paste

1 ½ mugs red lentils

4 mugs water

1 tin coconut milk

1 vegetable or chicken stock cube

Juice of ½ lime

2 tbsps. soy sauce

Coriander to serve

1. Heat the oil in a large pot, add the chopped onions, carrots and celery, fry on a medium heat for a few moments, add the curry paste and sliced lemon grass. Fry for a few minutes longer, then add the lentils, water, coconut milk and crumble in the stock cube.
2. Cook for 20mins.

3. Blitz to smooth with a hand blender or liquidizer, add a little more water if very thick. Add the lime juice and soy sauce, either stir through the chopped coriander or use as a garnish on the top.

Hints, Tips and Adaptations

Gluten free, dairy free, vegetarian if you use veg stock, freezable, microwavable.

If you can't get lemongrass, use a couple of strips of lemon peel.

Use parsley if you don't like coriander.

For less spicy soup, reduce the amount of curry paste.

Vegetable Paella

Serves 4 - 6

¾ mug paella rice

2 small onions, thinly sliced

1 red pepper, diced

100g green beans, topped & tailed, cut into 3cm long pieces

200g Brussels sprouts, quartered

1 small can chickpeas, drained

1 tin chopped tomatoes + 1 tin water

1 clove garlic, thinly sliced

1 glass white wine

½ tsp. ground turmeric

½ tsp. smoked paprika

1 tsp. paprika

2 tsps. vegetable stock powder

Pinch chilli flakes (optional)

1 tbsp. olive oil

1. Heat the oil in a large, shallow pan, add the onion and garlic, sizzle for a few minutes to soften but not brown.
2. Add the red pepper, stir to combine, then add the spices, chickpeas and rice. Stir well to coat the beans and grains with the spices.

3. Add the white wine, bubble to reduce, then add the tomatoes and the can of water.

4. Stir well, bring to the boil, turn down the heat to a simmer, put a lid on the pan and cook for 20mins.

5. Add the green beans and sprouts, cook for a further 12mins.

6. Season and serve.

Hints, Tips and Adaptations

Swap around the vegetables

Try using different beans

Vegetable & Pistachio Biryani

Serves 4

I like a biryani, the vegetable ones in particular are delicious and light

600g mixed vegetables eg. Cauliflower, broccoli, carrots, onions, celery, peppers etc.

¾ mug brown basmati rice

100g shelled pistachio nuts

3 cardamom pods

4 cloves

1 sm cinnamon stick

1 tsp. mustard seeds

1 tsp. ground coriander

½ tsp. ground turmeric

2 tsps. paprika

½ tsp. chilli powder

6 good desert spoons Greek yogurt

Salt & pepper

15g butter

Coriander or parsley to garnish

1. Bring a pan of water to the boil, pour in the rice and cook for 10mins. Drain and allow to steam.
2. Chop the vegetables into bite size pieces, heat 1 tbsp oil in a heavy based pan and fry for a few minutes to start the cooking process. Add

the pistachio nuts to the vegetables, then the spices. Stir well to combine, then add the yogurt. Remove from the heat and season.

3. Line the bottom of a large, heavy based pan with a circle of non-stick baking parchment. Place the pan on a low heat and put the butter on top of the parchment.

4. Sprinkle in a layer of rice, followed by a layer of vegetables. Continue until everything is used up. You should have at least 2 layers of each, maybe 3 depending on the size of your pan.

5. Increase the heat until you hear sizzling from the pan, reduce the heat to low, put a tight fitting lid onto the pan and allow the biryani to cook for 40 mins.

6. To serve, turn out onto a serving plate, remove the baking parchment and sprinkle with coriander or parsley.

Hints, Tips & Alternatives

Gluten free. For dairy free, use dairy free yogurt & butter.

Use mixed seasonal vegetables.

Use white rice instead of brown, reduce the cooking time to 30 mins.

Vegetable Wreath

Serves 8 to 12

This is a very impressive vegetarian dish, it would work not only as a Christmas day option, or party piece, but also as a standard family meal.

1 tin croissant dough

85g hazelnuts, chopped

85g green lentils

85g buckwheat

1 tin chopped tomatoes

1 tbsp. chopped rosemary

1 tbsp. oil + extra for drizzling

2 small onions, chopped

2 small red peppers, chopped

1 tbsp. mild curry powder

1 tsp. dried mixed herbs

1 egg

2 parsnips, sliced into 5mm pieces

3 carrots, sliced into 5mm pieces

2 beetroot, diced into 1cm pieces

Egg wash to glaze

1. Heat the oven to 200C/400F/Gas6

2. In a roasting tin, toss the carrots, parsnips and beetroot with salt, pepper and a drizzle of oil. Put into the oven for 30mins to roast.

3. Put the lentils and buckwheat in a pan with 1 mugful of water and the chopped rosemary. Bring to the boil, put a lid on the pan, reduce the heat and simmer for 20mins.

4. In another pan, heat 1 tbsp. oil over a medium high heat, add the chopped onions and peppers and fry until soft. Add the curry powder and mixed herbs, remove from the heat.

5. Stir in the hazelnuts, tinned tomatoes, cooked lentils and buckwheat, season to taste, allow to cool a little and stir through the egg.

6. Line a baking sheet with a piece of non-stick baking parchment.

7. Open the croissant dough, cut through the perforations and arrange the triangles of dough in a circle, on the baking sheet, slightly overlapping the wide ends and with the points of the triangles pointing outwards.

8. Spoon the lentil filling round inner edge of the croissant ring, arrange the roasted vegetables on top.

9. With a knife, cut 3 slashes through each of the croissant points, fold over the top of the ring of lentils and vegetables, pulling the slashes gently apart and tucking the point of the dough under the middle of the ring.

10. Brush the dough with egg wash, reduce the oven temperature to 180C/350/Gas4 and cook the wreath for 45mins.

Hints, Tips and Adaptations

Vegan if you replace the egg with a vegan substitute, vegetarian, gluten free if you use gluten free puff pastry. Dairy free

Freezable, keeps for a couple of days in the fridge. Re heat in an oven to keep the pastry crisp

Use different nuts – hazelnuts, walnuts, pecans or almonds for a different flavour.

Use red lentils instead of green lentils or buckwheat.

Use puff pastry instead of croissant dough.
Adding a teaspoon of oil to your egg wash will make the glaze shine more.

Mushrooms

All types of edible mushrooms contain varying degrees of protein and fibre. They also contain B vitamins and selenium.

Texturally, mushrooms are an excellent substitute for red meat and button mushrooms, when they are exposed to UV light, either indoors or outdoors are one of the few sources of non-animal vitamin D.

Wild mushrooms such as shiitake, oyster, chanterelle, porcini etc have different flavours, textures and nutritional values, they are often available dried, which also preserves their nutrients.

What to look for

Whether you are buying white button mushrooms or wild mushrooms, the caps should have a fresh unblemished look. Avoid any slimy, cracked or coarse looking mushrooms.

How to store

Ideally you want to buy mushrooms loose, store them in a paper bag or carton without a lid. If you leave mushrooms on your window sill, bottoms up for a couple of hours it will boost the vitamin D content.

How to prepare mushrooms

Wipe any grit or dirt from mushroom caps with a soft cloth or piece of kitchen paper, remove stalks if they are large, dirty or tough, the stalks can often be chopped up and used in the dish.

Large mushrooms like Portobello will be better peeled as the skin on top of the cap can be tough, just go around the edge of the cap and pull back the skin from the edge.

Mushroom caps can then be sliced, diced or left whole. Wild mushrooms like oyster and chanterelle are more fluted in shape and are better torn into pieces.

To reconstitute dried mushrooms, soak them in warm water for about 20 minutes, the strained soaking liquid has lots of flavour, so use it to make a sauce or gravy.

How to cook

There is nothing more delicious than mushrooms flash fried in a little butter, but research is showing that if mushrooms are microwaved or grilled, their antioxidant levels increase. The main thing is to cook them for a short time and don't boil them.

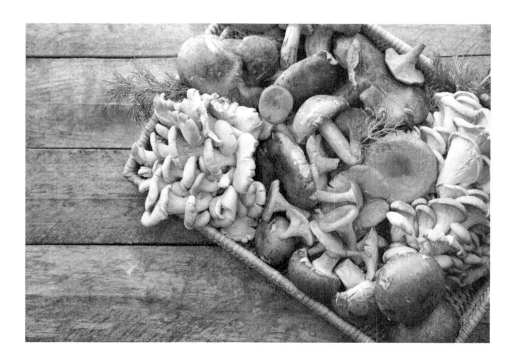

Stuffed Mushrooms with Hazelnuts

Serves 4

4 large flat mushrooms

2 tbsp olive oil

50g hazelnuts – roasted and the skins rubbed off

25g white bread crumbs

4 tbsp chopped parsley

1 clove garlic

50g Parmesan or other hard cheese

Zest of ½ lemon

1. Set the oven to 2ooC/400F/Gas6
2. Trim the stalks on the mushrooms, peel and drizzle with a little olive oil.
3. Put the bread, and parsley and garlic into a food processor and blitz to fine. Add the hazelnuts and blitz again to semi fine.
4. Transfer to a bowl, add the lemon zest, cheese and olive oil. Season with pepper.
5. Divide between the mushrooms and bake for 15 – 20 min.

Mushroom & Caper Crostini

Serves 2

1 tbsp. olive oil

100g mushrooms, sliced

½ tsp. fresh marjoram

1 small garlic clove – chopped

½ tbsp. capers

½ tbsp. chopped parsley

1 tbsp. Parmesan shavings

1 – 2 slices sourdough bread – toasted

1. Heat the oil in a frying pan, add the mushrooms, marjoram and garlic and cook over a medium heat stirring now and again.
2. Add the capers and parsley, increase the heat to boil off the liquid.
3. Season and spread onto slices of toast.

Mushroom Soup

Serves 4

30g butter

1 medium onion - chopped

340g mushrooms - chopped

3 tbsps. chopped parsley

1 small clove garlic – whole, skin removed

2 slices of bread (about 100g) – torn into pieces

900ml chicken or vegetable stock

½ tsp. grated nutmeg

75ml half fat crème fraiche (optional)

Salt & pepper to taste

1. Melt the butter in a large, heavy saucepan
2. Add the chopped onion and clove of garlic. Fry gently for a few minutes to soften.
3. Add the chopped mushrooms, increase the heat and when the juice starts to come out of the mushrooms, add the bread.
4. Stir round to allow the bread to absorb the mushroom juices, then add the stock.
5. Bring to the boil, turn down and simmer gently for 10 minutes.
6. Add the parsley, cream and grated nutmeg.

7. Taste and add salt and pepper as required.

Shiitake Mushroom Pate

Makes enough for 4 to 6 servings

This is a super tasty, super easy pate! Eat it on crackers or oatcakes, spread on toast or use as a dip.

250g shiitake mushrooms

3 tbsp toasted sunflower seeds

2 cloves garlic

Olive oil

1 tbsp soya sauce

1. Remove the woody stalks from the mushrooms, put the caps in a food processor and whiz with the toasted sunflower seeds and garlic.
2. Add a little olive oil if you want a stiffish mixture, or more if you're making a dip.
3. Add soya sauce and black pepper to taste.

Wild Mushroom Pithivier

Serves 6

600g mushrooms, cut or torn into pieces – I used a mixture of chestnut, chanterelle, shiitake & pied de mouton

500g puff pastry

300ml stock – vegetable or chicken

1 tbsp. dried porcini mushrooms

50g butter

1 medium onion, sliced

150ml crème fraiche

2 tbsps. marsala or sherry

1 tbsp. chopped tarragon

1 tbsp. chopped parsley

Egg wash to glaze

1. Heat a heavy based pan, add the stock and porcini mushrooms, bring to the boil, then transfer to a jug and set aside for the mushrooms to re-hydrate.

2. Add the butter to the pan, when foaming add the sliced onion and cook for a few minutes, stirring now and again until softened and slightly coloured. Add the fresh mushrooms to the pan and cook for a few minutes.

3. Strain the stock into the pan, chop the porcini mushrooms if necessary and add. Bring to the boil and simmer until the liquid has reduced by half.

4. Add the crème fraiche, stir from time to time and simmer until the liquid has reduced down to a thick sauce.

5. Add the marsala or sherry, tarragon and parsley. Simmer for a couple of minutes longer, then remove from the heat and cool completely.

6. Roll out the pastry to about 2mm thick. Cut 6 each, 9.5cm and 11cm rounds. Re-rolling the pastry scraps as necessary.

7. Divide the cooled mushroom mixture between the smaller pastry circles, leaving an approx 1cm margin all the way around. Dab a little water around the edge and cover with the larger piece of pastry, press the edges together and crimp with your fingers or the prongs of a fork.

8. Make a hole in the top of the pastry with a skewer to allow steam to escape. Brush with egg wash and then go around each pithivier with a knife, making crescent shaped scores from top to bottom, all the way around.

9. Heat the oven to 200C/400F/Gas6, bake the pithiviers for 20 to 30 mins or until the pastry is golden and crisp.

Beetroot

The purple packed superfood!

Available all year beetroot can be used in all sorts of dishes from casseroles, soups and dips to salads, cakes and drinks. It has a sweet, earthy flavour that you just know is doing your body good.

As with all fresh vegetables, they are low in calories and packed with nutrients, in particular folate, manganese, potassium, iron and vitamin C.

What to look for

As well as the dark red varieties, beetroot can also be golden, pink or white. It is usually sold with stems intact, so look for firm, smooth skinned roots with a bright colour and fresh tops. Anything soft, wizened or dull looking has been hanging around for a while.

How to prepare it

Quick and easy to prepare, just twist off the tops and scrub under the tap. Older and bigger beetroot can have a leathery ring of skin around the growing top and this can be pared off. The root can be nipped off with a sharp knife. The one thing that you don't particularly want to do is peel the roots as the colour tends to 'bleed', the skins are also very thin and can be eaten.

How to cook it

Beetroot can be boiled, roasted, stir fried or eaten raw

Boiling

You want to keep the root as intact as possible to avoid too much of the vegetable juice 'bleeding' into the water, so just pop the roots into a pot, add enough water just to cover, bring to the boil and simmer until tender. Once the roots are cooked, they can be used as they are, or the skins can be pinched off.

Roasting

This is my favourite way of cooking beetroot, just cut it into regular sized pieces, sprinkle with salt, pepper and a drizzle of oil. Toss and roast. The flavour intensifies and the colour stays put.

Stir frying

Raw beetroot can have a bitter edge to it and stir frying starts the cooking process and mellows the flavour. My favourite stir fry way with beetroot is to either cut it into thin match sticks or coarsely grate it, toss in a pan with a little butter or oil and the rind of an orange. Once it's hot, it's ready. Eat as a vegetable or toss through salad.

You can also stir fry in the Chinese sense with other vegetables, meat, rice or noodles. It will taste fantastic and everything in the pan will have a rosy glow!

Coping with stains

A beetroot stain is hard to eradicate. The main thing with any beetroot stain is to wash it out with cold water. Cold water is important so as not to 'cook' the stain in. You'll probably have to add some soap to a fabric or carpet stain, work fast to prevent the stain drying, rubbing and dabbing with a white cloth to lift as much of the stain as possible. If it's your hands or chopping board, again use cold water to rinse, then rub with salt and the cut side of half a lemon.

Here are a few of my favourite beetroot recipes, if you've been used to pickled beetroot, give them a try!

Beetroot, Chickpea & Coconut Curry

Serves 4

This is a great curry, not only is it made in one dish in the oven, it's also vegan/vegetarian and gluten free, not to mention delicious! Serve with rice, naan or roti.

1 large onion

600g beetroot, topped, tailed & cut into wedges

1 tin chickpeas, drained

2 cloves garlic, thinly sliced

5cm piece of ginger, finely grated

1 red chilli, chopped

1 heaped tsp ground cumin

1 heaped tsp ground coriander

1 heaped tsp ground ginger

½ tsp ground turmeric

1 tbsp vegetable oil

1 tsp salt

1 tin coconut milk

Chopped coriander or parsley to serve

1. Pre heat the oven to 200C/400F/ Gas6.

2. Put all the ingredients except the coconut milk into a roasting tin or oven proof dish. Put into the oven and roast for 40 minutes, turning the mixture with a spoon half-way though.

3. Pour over the coconut milk and bake for a further 10 minutes.

4. Remove from the oven, taste and adjust seasoning, stir through the coriander or parsley to serve.

Hints, Tips and Adaptations

Re heat in a microwave, gluten free, dairy free

Spice the curry up or down by adjusting the chilli

Swap the chickpeas for any other beans

Swap the beetroot for carrots

Beetroot Fritters

Makes 8

I made these for my teenage children one night when I was going out, thinking they would be enough for 4 and I would have some when I came home. They were completely scoffed & I ended up with a piece of toast!!

1 large beetroot

2 medium carrots

1 large onion

1 tsp. cumin seed

1 heaped tbsp horseradish sauce

100g chickpea flour

100ml water

Salt & pepper

Oil for frying

1. Coarsely grate the beetroot & carrots, finely slice the onion.
2. Mix with the cumin seed, horseradish sauce, chickpea flour, water, salt & pepper.
3. Heat about 5mm oil in a large heavy based frying pan, when hot, take handfuls of the vegetable mixture and put them in the pan. Fry on a medium hot heat for 5 mins each side. The oil should be hot enough to bubble and brown the fritters, but not hot enough to burn them.
4. Turn the fritters over and cook the other side for 5 mins.
5. Drain on kitchen paper.

6. These can now be eaten as they are or cooled and reheated in a preheated oven at 170C/325F/Gas3 for 15mins. Serve with cucumber raita

Hints, Tips and Adaptations

Dairy free, gluten free, nut free, microwavable, freezable

Try swapping in parsnips or swede.

Serve with spinach or cucumber raita.

Beetroot & Ginger Soup

Serves 6

This is a lighter soup for those spring days that are on the chilly side.

450g raw beetroot, topped, tailed & chopped

2 carrots, roughly chopped

2 small onions, roughly chopped

2 sticks celery, roughly chopped

2 medium potatoes, diced

1 tbsp. grated root ginger

2 tsps. ground ginger

1 ltr. vegetable stock

150ml half fat crème fraiche or double cream

Salt & pepper

1 tbsp. oil

1. Put the chopped beetroot, onion, carrot, celery & potatoes into a heavy based pan with the oil and fry gently for a few minutes to soften and start to colour.
2. Add the grated & ground ginger, stir and pour over the stock. Bring to the boil and simmer for 20 mins.
3. Blend with a stick blender or liquidiser, stir in most of the crème fraiche or cream, keeping a little back for garnish and adjust the seasoning.

4. Ladle into bowls, swirl through an extra teaspoon of cream and sprinkle with a few chopped chives.

Hints Tips & Adaptations

Gluten free, to make dairy free omit the crème fraiche, add a spoonful of dairy free yogurt to each bowl. Freezable without the cream. Re-heat in a microwave.

Vegetarian with vegetable stock.

Don't be tempted to use cooked, vac packed beetroot, the colour will fade.

Beetroot Hummus

Serves 4 – 6

My kids have loved this since they were little. If you have beetroot haters, try them with this!

200g approx., raw beetroot (about 4) cut into 6 wedges if big

1 small onion – cut into wedges

½ can of chickpeas or beans

1 small red chilli (or to taste)

1 small garlic clove

1 tbsp. maple syrup

1 tsp. ground coriander

1 tsp. ground cumin

2 tbsps. mayonnaise

2 spring onions – finely sliced

50g/¼ block feta cheese

1 handful toasted crushed hazelnuts

1. Make a piece of tin foil approx. 50cm long. Put the beetroot wedges, onion & garlic in the middle of the tin foil, drizzle with a little oil, sprinkle with salt & pepper. Fold up the foil to make a parcel. Place on a baking sheet and roast in the oven for 30min.

2. Remove foil parcel from the oven, open carefully, test to see if the beetroot is tender. Return to the oven if not, or if cooked, tip the contents into the bowl of a food processor.

3. Add the chilli, ground coriander, ground cumin & chick peas. Blitz to puree.

4. Add the mayonnaise and maple syrup, blitz again, taste for seasoning.

5. Pile on to a serving plate, sprinkle with feta cheese, hazelnuts & spring onions.

Roasted Root Soup

Serves 4 to 6

I love the colour of this soup – beetroot pink! Use a combination of whatever roots you have in the fridge.

1.5Kg mixed root vegetables – I used 2 potatoes, 2 beetroot, 3 carrots, 2 onions, 1 sweet potato, ¼ turnip and ¼ celeriac.

Drizzle of oil

Salt & pepper

Vegetable stock to cover

1 tsp. fresh thyme

1. Pre-heat the oven to 200C/400/Gas6
2. Cut the vegetables into bite size pieces, drizzle over a little oil, salt & pepper, give everything a good mix. Put in the oven for 45 mins.
3. Once cooked, transfer the vegetables to a large pot, add the stock and thyme, bring to the boil. Simmer for 10 mins, then blitz with a hand blender. Check seasoning and serve.

Hints, Tips and Variations

Wheat, gluten & dairy free
Freezable, re heat in a microwave.
Make this soup vegetarian/vegan friendly by using vegetable stock or water.
Use rosemary instead of thyme.

Spicy Beetroot Spaghetti

Serves 1

2 small beetroot (135g)

1 tomato (150g)

1 small red onion

3cm piece spicy chorizo

1 tsp. balsamic vinegar

½ tsp. chopped thyme leaves

1 small clove garlic

Glug of olive oil

Salt & pepper to taste

Parsley to garnish

1. Spiralise, shred or coarsely grate the beetroot.
2. Cut the tomato & chorizo into approx. 1cm dice, thinly slice the onion, finely slice the garlic.
3. Heat the oil in a heavy based frying pan, add the onion & garlic, fry for a couple of minutes, then add the chorizo. Fry for a few moments and add the tomato.
4. Cook the tomato until it starts to break down, add the beetroot, stir to heat through, then add the thyme and balsamic vinegar.
5. Stir everything together, taste & adjust seasoning
6. Tip into a bowl, sprinkle with the parsley and serve.

Root Vegetables

Carrots, parsnips, swede

Carrots are another vegetable staple along with onions and celery. Whether you're making soup, a casserole or stock, those three veg will give you flavour and nutrients galore.

Carrots have a very high proportion of vitamin A and other minerals. A freshly juiced glass of carrot juice will not only help with skin health, but also provide immune protection.

Parsnips and Swede

These two are mainly starchy vegetables with a good mixture of nutrients including B vitamins, vitamins A & C as well as potassium. They are always cooked, either steamed, baked, roasted or mashed. If using them in soup or casserole I'm usually careful not to use too much as they can give a taste to a dish or a 'nippy' edge.

Carrot, Ginger & Rosemary Soup

Serves about 8

This is a nice autumn soup. Warming with the ginger, filling with the lentils, but still light enough in warmer weather.

1 tbsp. oil

1 leek, sliced

500g carrots, sliced

100g root ginger, finely grated

120g red lentils

Approx. 1.5ltr vegetable stock

1 tsp chopped rosemary

50ml double cream

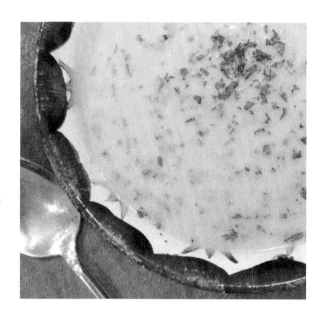

1. Heat the oil in a heavy based pan, add the sliced leek and carrots, fry on a medium heat for a few minutes to soften the vegetables a little.
2. Add the grated ginger, stir everything together, then pour in the stock, lentils and chopped rosemary.
3. Stir again, bring to the boil, put a lid on the pan and simmer for 20 mins.
4. Blend the soup with a stick blender and stir through the cream. Adjust the seasoning and serve.

Hints, Tips and Adaptations

Dairy free if you miss out the cream, gluten free, nut free, microwavable. Freezable without the cream.

Vegetarian if you use vegetable stock.

Try thyme instead of rosemary.

Celeriac

Celeriac is the knobbly vegetable in the supermarket that no-one knows what to do with. It's actually a very versatile and nutritious vegetable with a mild celery/parsley flavour.

Closely related to celery, celeriac is grown for its bulbous root rather than it's stems, it is a good source of fibre, B vitamins, vitamin C, Vitamin K, phosphorus and potassium.

So What Can I Do With It...

Being a root vegetable, celeriac can be used in the same way as any other root - roasted, steamed, mashed, pureed.... It can be used as a celery alternative in soups, stews and salads. Celeriac will discolour once you've cut it, so soak it in water with a little lemon juice to prevent it going brown around the edges.

How do I Prepare It...

The skin of celeriac is quite thick and tough, it's also a knobbly vegetable so can harbour dirt. The best way prepare it is:

1. Wash under running water and give it a scrub with a vegetable brush to remove as much earth as possible.
2. Cut the top and bottom off the root - this gives you a flat base to work from.
3. Cut around and down the sides until all the skin and rooty bits are removed.
4. You can now use the celeriac in whatever form you wish - cubed, sliced, batons or grated.

5. If you want to do something with all the peelings, they give a fantastic, flavoured stock. Just cover with water, simmer for 20min, strain and use the liquid in soups, stews, etc.

Celeriac, Apple and Thyme Soup

Serves 6

This soup surprised me, I didn't think I would like it, I've never enjoyed savoury with sweet flavours! It's also very white and I like dishes with a bit of colour. Serve it in a brightly coloured bowl, the cheese finishes it perfectly.

1 large celeriac root

1 medium onion

1 tbsp. fresh thyme leaves

2 sticks celery

1 tbsp. oil

Approx. 750ml chicken or vegetable stock

1 small cooking apple

1 medium eating apple

100ml double cream

120g strong cheese, eg. Cheddar or stilton, grated

1. Scrub the celeriac root, cut off the skin and cut into chunks.
2. Put the celeriac peelings into the stock and bring to the boil. Simmer while you prepare the remaining ingredients.
3. Roughly chop the onion and celery, heat the oil in a large pot and fry gently with the diced celeriac.
4. Peel, core and roughly chop the apples add to the pan with the thyme and strain in the stock. Bring to the boil, simmer for 20mins.

5. Puree with a hand blender or liquidiser, add the cream and season to taste.

6. To serve, put 20g grated cheese in the bottom of a bowl and ladle over the soup. Serve with crusty bread.

Hints, Tips and Adaptations

Gluten free, vegetarian if you use vegetable stock, freezable before adding cream, microwavable.

Make sure you use strong cheese, or you won't taste it. As well as cheddar or stilton, try any strong cheese that melts well.

Celeriac, Lentil & Hazelnut Salad

Serves 4

60g hazelnuts

200g Puy, green or beluga lentils (1 mugful)

2 bay leaves

Sprig of rosemary - chopped

1 small celeriac (about 650g) – peeled & cut into bite size chunks

3 tbsps. olive oil

2 tbsps. cider vinegar

1 tsp. Dijon mustard

2 tbsps. tarragon

4 tbsps. parsley

Salt & pepper to taste

Mixed leaves to serve

1. Simmer the lentils in an equal quantity of water with the bay leaves and rosemary for 15 to 20min or until just tender.
2. Mix the olive oil, cider vinegar, Dijon mustard & tarragon together to make a dressing. Season with salt & pepper.
3. Once the lentils are cooked, remove the bay leaves and drain any excess water. Stir the dressing into the lentils while they are still hot.
4. Steam the celeriac until tender (about 10 min)

5. Roast the hazelnuts at 180C/350F/Gas5 for about 10min. Remove from the oven, cool and remove any loose skins by rubbing them between your hands. Chop roughly.

6. Stir the warm lentils, celeriac & half the hazelnuts together with the parsley.

7. To serve, toss through the mixed leaves and either serve in a bowl or divide onto individual plates. Garnish with the remaining hazelnuts.

Celeriac Mash

Adding celeriac to potatoes to make a mash reduces the calories drastically. 100g celeriac has just over 14 calories, whereas 100g potatoes has just over 71 calories. By mixing the two, you reduce your calories, but increase flavour without having to add butter or milk to make the potato spreadable.

Makes as much as you like!

1/3 celeriac root, peeled & roughly chopped

2/3 floury potates, peeled and roughly chopped

Salt & pepper to taste

1. Put the potatoes into a pot with a lid. Add enough water to just cover and put the celeriac on top. The idea is to boil the potatoes, but steam the celeriac. Bring to the boil and simmer until the potatoes are cooked.
2. Drain well, mash and add salt and pepper to taste.

Celeriac Slaw

Celeriac is good ingredient in coleslaw. I think it looks best teamed up with colourful veg! This salad is even better the next day once the celeriac and cabbage have softened and the flavours have had a chance to mingle.

¼ celeriac root, peeled and cut into fine shreds

¼ red cabbage, finely sliced

1 carrot, coarsley grated

1 red apple, cored & cubed

2 tbsp mayonnaise

2 tbsp Greek yogurt

1 tsp horseradish sauce

Squeeze of lemon juice

Salt & pepper

Chives (optional)

1. Put all the ingredients into a bowl and mix well to combine. Pile into a bowl and sprinkle with snipped chives to finish.

Coconut Dhal with Roasted Vegetables

Serves 4

This is a delicious dhal, we like it with lots of extra roasted vegetables.

200g yellow split peas

100g split red lentils

½ tsp ground turmeric

½ tsp ground cumin

1 can coconut milk

1 can water

Pinch of chilli flakes (optional)

1. Put all the above ingredients in a pan with a lid. Bring to the boil and simmer gently for about 40mins, or until the yellow split peas are tender.

I medium onion, chopped

2 large tomatoes, chopped

1 clove garlic, thinly sliced

1 cm piece of root ginger, grated

1 tsp black onion seeds

1 tsp oil

2. Heat the oil in a heavy based pan, add the onion seeds and when they begin to pop, add the onion, garlic and ginger. Stir and cook for a few minutes, then add the tomato. Bring to a simmer and cook for 10mins.

½ butternut squash, peeled and cut into 2cm cubes

4 medium beetroot, topped, tailed and cut into wedges

1 small head broccoli, floretted

1 tbsp. oil

3. Heat the oven to 200C/400F/Gas6, put the squash and beetroot into a roasting tin, season with salt & pepper and drizzle over 1 tbsp oil. Cook for approx. 30mins or until tender.
4. Place the broccoli florets on top of the dhal for the last 10 minutes of cooking.
5. To serve, stir the tomato mixture into the dhal and broccoli, divide onto plates and top with the roasted vegetables.

Hints, Tips and Variations

Gluten free, dairy free, vegetarian, vegan, freezable, reheat in a microwave.
Use any combination of vegetables for roasting – carrots, celeriac, courgette, parsnip, cauliflower…
Swap the yellow split peas for green ones

Cream of Roasted Squash, Carrot & Rosemary Soup

Serves 6

I don't often make a cream soup, but sometimes carrots need something to give them body and make them less 'carroty'. I don't particularly like carrot & orange or carrot & coriander soup, so I cooked them here with squash to give thickness and rosemary for flavour. The cream just finishes the soup nicely.

600g squash, peeled & cubed

600g carrots, scrubbed & sliced

1 onion, roughly chopped

1 ltr vegetable stock

10g rosemary leaves, chopped

100ml double cream

Salt & pepper

1. Heat the oven to 200C/400F/Gas6
2. Put the onion, squash & carrots into a roasting tin, drizzle with oil, sprinkle over salt & pepper and toss to coat everything. Put into the oven and roast for 20mins. Remove stir everything round and roast for another 10mins.

3. Tip the roasted vegetables into a large pot, add the stock and rosemary. Bring to the boil and simmer for 10 mins.

4. Puree with a blender, add the cream, bring back to the boil and check the seasoning before serving.

Hints, Tips and Adaptations

Gluten free, freezable, reheat in a microwave

Try using thyme or parsley instead of rosemary.

Nut Rissoles

Makes 8

These are delicious vegetable burgers, eat them with or without a bun. The spinach raita is a great sauce to eat with them. Again, either in or out of a bun.

650g mixed vegetables – eg. Carrots, celery, onion, leek, fennel, pepper, celeriac, squash, broccoli, cauliflower…

100g chopped mixed nuts

100g breadcrumbs

1 egg or 2 tbsp flax powder

1 tsp. curry powder

1 tsp. dried mixed herbs

Salt & pepper

Flour for dusting – I used gram flour in the photo, but wholemeal spelt or rye also works well.

Oil for frying

1. Chop the vegetables roughly, put into the bowl of a food processor and blitz until they resemble coarse breadcrumbs.
2. Tip into a mixing bowl, add the breadcrumbs, egg or flax powder, curry powder, mixed herbs, salt & pepper. Mix everything together well and allow the mixture to sit for 10mins.
3. Divide into 8 portions, press the mixture together to form patties. Coat well with flour.

4. Heat about 5mm oil in a large frying pan, when a piece of rissole, dropped into the oil sizzles, it's hot enough. Fry the rissoles in two batches, approx. 5mins each side, then drain on kitchen paper.

5. Eat hot with spinach raita or cool & either refrigerate or freeze for use later. Re-heat, at 180C/350F/Gas5 for 15 to 20 mins on a baking sheet.

Spinach Raita

300g fresh or 2 blocks frozen leaf spinach

1dstsp oil

1 tsp cumin seeds

½ tsp mustard seed

350ml natural yoghurt

1 tsp red chilli paste or to taste

salt and pepper

1. If using frozen spinach, defrost, squeeze out the water from the blocks and chop finely. If using fresh spinach, steam in a little water, drain, squeeze out the water between 2 plates and chop finely. Allow to cool.
2. Heat the oil in a small pan and fry the cumin and mustard seeds until they start to pop. Tip into a bowl and allow to cool.
3. Mix the yoghurt, toasted seeds, chilli paste and spinach together, season with salt and pepper. Chill until ready to serve.

Hints, Tips and Adaptations

Dairy free if you use dairy free yogurt, gluten free if you use gluten free breadcrumbs and flour, nut free if you swap the nuts for soya mince, a tin of beans or chickpeas.

Microwavable, freezable.

Potatoes and Swede au Gratin

Serves 8

1 large onion – sliced

300g swede – peeled, quartered and sliced

400g large potatoes – sliced (about 3)

handful of chopped parsley

2 tbsps. flour

200ml chicken or vegetable stock - hot

drizzle of double cream

40g grated cheddar/Parmesan cheese

1 tbsp. oil

knob of butter

1. Pre heat the oven to 180C/gas4
2. Heat the oil and butter in a pan, add the onion and garlic and fry until soft. Remove from the heat
3. In a bowl, mix the sliced potato and swede with the onions and garlic. Toss with the flour and parsley and season well.
4. Transfer to a large oven proof dish, pour over the stock and cream. Cover with tin foil and bake for 30 min.
5. After 30 min, remove the tin foil, sprinkle over the cheese and bake for further 20 – 30 min.

Rocket Burgers with Tomato Salsa

Makes 6 burgers

Rocket has a spicy flavour but is not just for salads. You could also use watercress, spinach, kale or nettles. I served these with baked potatoes, but you could also put them in buns.

1 pack rocket (60g)

1 ½ tins or mugfuls of cooked beans

3 spring onions, chopped

2 tbsps. soy sauce

2 tsps. ground cumin

1 tbsp. root ginger, finely grated

3 cloves garlic

1 tbsp. tahini or peanut butter

1 egg

4 tbsps. oatmeal or rolled oats, plus extra for coating.

Salt and pepper

Oil for frying

1. Put the rocket and beans into a food processor and pulse to roughly chop and blend together.
2. Add the spring onions, soy sauce, cumin, root ginger, garlic cloves, tahini and egg. Pulse again to mix, then add the oatmeal, salt & pepper.

Pulse again, the mixture should be dry enough to stick together, if it's too wet, add some extra oats.

3. Divide the mixture into 6 and form into patties. Roll in more oats to coat.

4. Heat about 1cm depth of oil in a large frying pan, when the oil is hot enough to sizzle when a flake of oats is dropped into it, fry the burgers for approx. 5mins each side.

5. Drain on kitchen paper once browned and crisp.

Make the salsa

2 large tomatoes

4 spring onions

1 tsp chilli flakes (optional)

Juice of ½ lime

1. Cut the tomatoes into 5mm cubes, finely slice the spring onions. Mix them together with the chilli flakes and lime juice.

2. Serve with the burgers either on the side or in a bun.

Hints, Tips and Adaptations

Gluten free if you use gluten free oats, dairy free, vegetarian, burgers are freezable, microwavable.

Use any tinned or dried beans

Spice the salsa up or down depending on the amount of chilli you use.

Skinny Dauphinoise Potatoes

Serves 4

There's nothing more delicious than garlicky, creamy dauphinoise potatoes. I've tweeked them here to make them less calorific & faster to cook but no less delicious.

800g floury potatoes – I used Maris Piper

1 medium onion, thinly sliced

2 cloves of garlic, thinly sliced

300ml chicken stock

100ml double cream

½ tsp. grated nutmeg

50g strong cheese, Gruyere or cheddar

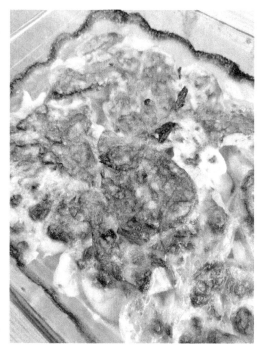

1. Heat the oven to 180C/350F/Gas4.
2. Slice the potatoes into 5mm slices. Put into a pan with the stock, cream, sliced onion and garlic. Grate in the nutmeg and bring to the boil. Simmer for 10 minutes, stirring now and again,
3. Spoon into an oven proof dish, being careful not to break up the potatoes too much and trying to arrange them in an even layer.
4. Season the liquid left in the pan with salt and pepper to taste, then pour over the potatoes.

5. Sprinkle over the cheese, put into the oven and bake uncovered for 45 minutes to 1 hour. The creamy liquid in the potatoes should reduce and thicken, but not go dry.

Hints Tips & Adaptations

Gluten free, to make dairy free, omit the cream and use extra stock. Microwave to re-heat

Try adding sliced celeriac, swede, sweet potato or squash with the potatoes for a different flavour.

Sweet Potato Linguine

Serves 1

1 small sweet potato (135g)

1 tomato (150g)

2 spring onions

25g pistachio nuts

1 tsp. chopped parsley

½ tsp. chopped thyme leaves

Zest of ¼ lemon + a squeeze of juice

1 small clove garlic

Glug of olive oil

Salt & pepper to taste

1. Spiralise, shred or coarsely grate the sweet potato & drizzle with a squeeze of lemon juice.
2. Cut the tomato into approx. 1cm dice, thinly slice the spring onion, crush the pistachio nuts, finely slice the garlic.
3. Heat the oil in a heavy based frying pan, add the tomato & garlic, fry for a couple of minutes until the tomato starts to break down.
4. Add the sweet potato, stir to heat through, then add the spring onion, herbs, lemon zest and ¾ of the pistachio nuts.
5. Stir to heat through, taste & adjust seasoning
6. Tip into a bowl, sprinkle with the remaining nuts and serve.

Vegetable Bouillon

Makes enough for 2 x 340g jars

125g salt

500g fresh vegetables

100g fresh herbs

2 large cloves garlic – peeled

1. Roughly chop the vegetables and put into the bowl of a food processor with the herbs, garlic and salt. Whizz until it is a well-blended granular paste.

2. Divide into 2 sterilised jars with vinegar proof lids, store in the fridge.

   I used carrots, celery, leeks and spring onions for my vegetable mix and rosemary, thyme, parsley, chives and tarragon for herbs.

   Other vegetables which could be used include onions, fennel, parsnips, turnip, beetroot, celeriac, peppers – you want vegetables that have a good flavour.

   If you very the kinds of herbs your stock will take on different flavours, the woody herbs of rosemary, thyme and sage are good staples as their flavour will last longer. Other herbs to try are bay leaves, oregano, dill, basil, mint and coriander.

   Use about 2 tsp per 500ml water

Asparagus is a spring vegetable...

The shoot (spear) of a fern-like plant, harvested over a period of around 8 weeks. The warmer the weather the faster the spears grow and after the harvesting period is finished, the plant is allowed to grow and replenish itself for the next season.

Purple, Green or White?

Asparagus varieties are either green or purple, white spears have been blanched by excluding them from sunlight, usually by heaping soil around the spears. This gives the spears a delicate flavour.

How Good Is It For Me?

Asparagus is a very low-calorie vegetable, having only 20 calories per 100g. It is also very nutritious, being high in folates, B vitamins, vitamin K, antioxidants and minerals. It has a reputation as a diuretic and aphrodisiac.

How Do I Prepare & Cook Asparagus?

Asparagus spears are harvested by cutting them just below the ground. The stems can be woody near the bottom and the advice is to snap the bottoms off, you'll waste a lot of your precious asparagus spears this way, I use a potato peeler to peel the skin off the bottom 2 or 3 centimetres of the spears and slice off the dry ends.

Asparagus is delicious cooked in many different ways, start very simply with steamed or griddled asparagus brushed with a little butter, it's also good barbecued. Try it on toast with poached or scrambled eggs. Serve it with Hollandaise or Bearnaise sauce. Wrap spears individually in pancetta or Parma ham before baking - these are good dipped into soft boiled eggs instead of toast soldiers!

If you want to be a bit more adventurous, wrap spears in boiled ham, roll up in a crepe pancake and top with cheese sauce. Try baking them into a tart or souffle, adding them to risotto, making them into a soup, sauce or pie.

Don't forget a salad - the options are endless here, the spears can be blanched or eaten raw, tossed with a mustard dressing, combined other salad ingredients, stirred into couscous or quinoa....

What Combinations Go Best With Asparagus?

Asparagus has quite a mild flavour and is very versatile, eat with eggs for a nutrition packed meal or combine with the rich flavours of ham, bacon and chorizo, all sorts of strongly flavoured cheeses, anchovies, smoked fish and herbs. Herbs that go particularly well are dill, tarragon and chives.

Asparagus Soup

Serves 4

1 bunch of asparagus – stems cut into 2cm pieces, tips reserved

1 medium onion - chopped

1 medium floury potato – peeled & chopped

Pinch of ground turmeric

500ml chicken or vegetable stock

25g butter

Small bunch of parsley

Drizzle of cold pressed olive or rapeseed oil (optional)

2 tsps. finely shredded mint leaves (optional)

Drizzle of double cream (optional)

1. Melt the butter in a heavy based pan, add the onion & fry gently for a few minutes to soften. Add the cubed potato and continue cooking for another few minutes.
2. Add the chopped asparagus spears to the pan, stir everything together and cook for a few minutes. Stir in the turmeric and allow to cook for a few seconds.
3. Stir in the stock, bring to the boil, put a lid on the pan and simmer for 15mins. In the last 2 minutes of cooking time, add the chopped parsley.
4. Roughly slice the asparagus tips.
5. Puree with a hand blender or liquidiser, then add the asparagus tips to the pan.
6. Season to taste, add cream if you would like.

7. Serve with a drizzle of oil and a sprinkling of mint leaves.

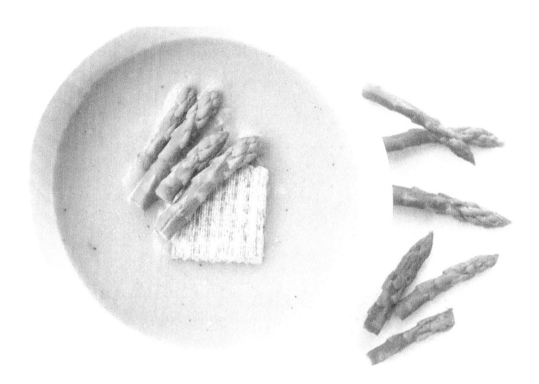

Avocado

Avocados are unique among the fruits in that they are a very concentrated food, more like a nut than a fruit. They are high in calories – one average avocado has about 300 calories and about 30grams of fat, as well as 12 grams of carbohydrate and 4 to 5 grams of protein.

Avocados are fairly high in most of the B vitamins, have a good amount of vitamins A, C and E, are rich in potassium and have good amounts of magnesium, iron and manganese.

What to look for

Avocados come in two main types, a bright green, thin skinned variety, or a rough, thicker skinned variety that turns brown as it ripens. Both varieties have pale green, mild, smooth flesh.

Both varieties are ready to use when they yield if gently pressed, although it's easier to tell when the rougher skinned avocados are ready because the skin starts to turn brown.

How to prepare it

The easiest way to prepare an avocado is to run a knife length ways from the stalk end, down, round the bottom and back up to the stalk end again. The blade of the knife will rest against the large stone in the middle of the fruit. Once you have a cut all the way around, twist the two halves and they will separate. To remove the stone, whack your knife into the stone and twist. If you have a ripe avocado, it will just lift out.

You can now scoop the flesh out with a spoon, slice or dice the flesh with a knife and squeeze the skin together to remove the flesh. Or, if you have a thin-skinned avocado, quarter it and carefully peel back the skin. The flesh can now be sliced, diced or mashed as required.

How to use it

As a child I remember when avocados were an exotic treat. My mother used to either pile prawn cocktail into the centre where the stone had been or dice it up with kiwi fruit, melon and French dressing.

A half avocado sprinkled with salt & pepper and served with a spoonful of French dressing makes a delicious, snack, along with mashed avocado on toast or half an avocado, sprinkled with Parmesan cheese and grilled for a few minutes.

Guacamole is a great way to eat it or try   blending it into a smoothie for a creamy result.

How to ripen an avocado

If you end up with a really hard avocado, putting it into a paper bag with a ripe banana will soften it up in a couple of days.

If you can't wait that long, wrap the avocado in foil, heat the oven to 90C, put the wrapped avocado into the oven for 10 minutes. Remove and put into the fridge for 10 minutes, unwrap and use as needed.

Avocado & Soft Boiled Egg Salad

Serves 1

This is another winning combination, an easy, healthy supper if you're on your own.

1 handful of romaine or gem lettuce

Small handful rocket leaves

6 cherry tomatoes, halved

½ avocado, cut into pieces

1 egg

1 tsp. chopped chives

1 tsp. chopped mint leaves

3 tsps. Dijon dressing

1. Boil the egg for 4 minutes if medium or 5 minutes if large. Run under cold running water to cool before peeling and cutting into quarters.
2. Slice the romaine or gem lettuce and toss with the rocket leaves, avocado, cherry tomatoes and half the herbs.
3. Arrange the egg over the top of the salad, sprinkle over the remaining herbs and drizzle over the dressing to serve.

Dijon Dressing

This is a useful dressing to have in the cupboard, it goes with almost any salad and also works with steamed vegetables such as new potatoes, carrots, beans and asparagus.

Makes about 150ml

100ml olive, rapeseed, vegetable or sunflower oil

50ml cider or white wine vinegar

1 tsp dried mixed herbs

1 tsp Dijon mustard

Good pinch of salt

Grind of black pepper

Pinch of caster sugar

1. Put everything into a 225ml jar with a lid and shake well. Taste and adjust the seasoning as necessary.

Hints, Tips and Adaptations

Gluten free, dairy free

Use different herbs to change the flavour

Try a drizzle of cold pressed oil and balsamic syrup instead of the dressing.

Use duck or quails eggs instead of hens.

Avocado, Harissa & Rosemary Roasted Tomatoes on Toast

Avocado on toast has become a staple, the secret is to pile it high & include lots of flavours!

Serves 2

1 medium ripe avocado

1 tbsp lemon juice

2 slices good bread

1 tsp harissa paste

12 cherry tomatoes

1 small red onion thinly sliced

½ tsp chopped rosemary

Drizzle olive oil

Salt & pepper

Chives or parsley to finish

1. Preheat the oven to 200C/400F/Gas6
2. Put the sliced onion, cherry tomatoes & rosemary into an oven proof dish, drizzle with olive oil, sprinkle with salt & pepper and mix well. Put into the oven and roast for 20 minutes.
3. Run a knife lengthways around the avocado, remove the stone and scoop out the flesh onto a dinner plate. Season with salt & pepper, drizzle over the lemon juice and mash with a fork. Try not to mash the avocado too smoothly, it's good with some chunky bits.

4. Toast the bread and spread a little harissa over each piece. Divide the smashed avocado between the two pieces of toast and roughly level. Top with the roasted tomatoes and onions and sprinkle over a few finely chopped chives or parsley. (I used chive flowers for the picture)

Hints, Tips & Adaptations

Use gluten free bread if necessary.

Try to use sourdough or good wholemeal bread rather than white sliced loaf.

There are lots of other toppings you could use instead of roasted tomatoes. Try bacon, smoked salmon, cured meat or poached, fried or scrambled egg.

Avocado & Garlic Mushrooms on Toast

Garlic mushrooms and avocado are a really tasty combination, add lots of punchy flavours for a special meal.

Serves 2

1 medium ripe avocado

1 tbsp lemon juice

2 slices good bread

1 tsp horseradish sauce

250g mushrooms, thinly sliced

1 tsp thyme leaves

1 tsp grated lemon rind

2 cloves garlic, finely chopped

1 tsp porcini mushroom powder (optional)

Drizzle of truffle oil (optional)

1 tsp grated nutmeg

1 Tbsp olive oil

Finely chopped chives or parsley

Salt & pepper

1. Heat the olive oil in a heavy based frying pan, add the garlic, thyme leaves and lemon rind. Sizzle gently for a few moments until the garlic begins to turn golden.
2. Add the sliced mushrooms and cook on a higher heat, stirring from time to time until all the watery mushroom juice has evaporated. Sprinkle

over the porcini powder, grated nutmeg. Remove from the heat and drizzle with a little truffle oil. Season with salt & pepper.

3. Toast the bread, spread with horseradish sauce and divide the smashed avocado between the slices. Top with the mushroom mixture and finish with a sprinkle of parsley or finely chopped chives.

Hints, Tips & Adaptations

Use gluten free bread if necessary.

Try to use sourdough or good wholemeal bread rather than white sliced loaf.

Porcini mushroom powder is a useful addition to your spice cupboard. Sprinkle a little onto any mushroom dish to give extra flavour. It's easy to make – just whizz dried porcini mushrooms in a blender until they have turned to powder. Tip back into the jar and use as required.

Minty Guacamole

Serves 2

1 medium ripe avocado

1 spring onion, finely sliced

Juice of ½ lime

2 tbsp coriander, roughly chopped

1 tbsp mint leaves, roughly chopped

Pinch of salt and pepper

1. Halve the avocado, remove the stone and scoop the flesh into a bowl. Mash a little with a fork. It should be smoothish, with some chunks for texture.
2. Add the finely sliced spring onion, chopped mint, coriander, salt & pepper and lime juice. Mix everything together well.
3. Pile into a dish to serve.

Salads and Herbs

Salad leaves come in all sorts of shapes, colours and flavours. Whether you like 'head' salad like iceberg, romaine, gem or butter lettuce, mild leaves like spinach and corn salad, or go for more peppery flavours of watercress, rocket or mustard greens, dark coloured leaves are richer in chlorophyll, vitamin A and folic acid. All salads are also good fibre foods and contain varying amounts of calcium, potassium and iron.

Spicy and bitter leaves have the reputation of being good blood cleansers

Herbs add flavour and interest for any dish, can give a plain recipe a new dimension and can be divided into two categories; woody and soft.

Woody herbs, rosemary, thyme, sage and bay are good used in casseroles or dishes cooked for longer times. They are often used more sparingly. Woody herbs are usually shrubby

Soft herbs, parsley, coriander, mint, tarragon, chives, dill, basil, oregano are best for short cooking times, used in salads or sprinkled on a dish at the last minute and can be used more abundantly. Soft herbs tend to be sown annually and die once winter sets in.

What to look for

Bright, crisp salad and herbs, no brown bits, wilted leaves or mushiness.

How to store

Packaged salad and herbs are best kept in the fridge wrapped in the packaging they were bought in. Try to use it within a couple of days of buying.

Keep 'head' lettuce attached to the stem and tear off or slice leaves as you need them. They will stay crisp far longer than removing the leaves and storing separately.

Bunches of herbs are sometimes sold un packaged and they can look a bit tired. Take a bunch home, cut a couple of centimetres off the bottom of the stalks and put into a jug of water. Like cut flowers they will perk up within a couple of hours.

How to use

The days of iceberg lettuce served with cucumber slices and tomato wedges is really over. Make your salad interesting by using a variety of leaf colours, textures and flavours, add chopped herbs for flavour and a simple dressing. If you're making the salad as a meal in itself, add extra vegetable elements.

Roast Squash Salad

Serves 2

200g Squash – peeled

¼ tsp vegetable bouillon

¼ tsp curry powder

1 tsp each pumpkin, sunflower & pinenuts

Handful mixed leaves

4 cherry tomatoes (30g)

½ tsp soy sauce

Drizzle oil

Squeeze of lemon juice

Salt & pepper

1. Pre-heat the oven to 190C/375F/Gas5.
2. Cut the squash into approx. 1cm cubes.
3. Toss with the oil, veg bouillon, curry powder, salt & pepper. Place on a roasting tin & roast for 20 – 30 min or until soft & browned around the edges.
4. Toast the seeds in a dry pan. When golden, remove from the heat and add the soy sauce to the hot pan, shaking the pan until the liquid has evaporated and the seeds are coated with a soy crust. Set aside.

5. Half the cherry tomatoes and toss with the leaves, when the squash is ready toss it into the leaves straight from the oven, sprinkle over the seeds and serve with a squeeze of lemon juice.

6. If serving cold, allow the squash to cool before adding to the salad.

Salade Nicoise

Serves 2

A Nicoise salad can contain almost any seasonal ingredient, including tuna, potatoes, cucumber, capers, artichokes, broad beans & the ingredients below. Choose ingredients depending on their freshness and colour. You want a good mixture.

2 eggs

50g green beans

1 small green pepper

3 medium on the vine tomatoes

1 spring onion

2 radishes

2 – 4 anchovies

A few basil leaves

Handful of black olives

1 clove garlic

Drizzle of olive oil

1. Steam the green beans for a few minutes until tender. Remove from the heat and refresh under cold running water. Drain & set aside.
2. Hard boil the eggs, then peel and quarter.
3. De-seed and slice the pepper into 5mm strips.
4. Quarter the tomatoes, remove any fibrous cores.

5. Thinly slice the spring onion

6. Slice the radishes

7. To make up the salad, use a flat plate, halve the garlic lengthways and rub the cut side over the surface of the plate. Layer up the green beans, tomato wedges & green pepper slices. Top with the egg quarters, a sprinkle of spring onion, a few olives and tear over the anchovies and basil leaves. Finish with a drizzle of olive oil.

Spinach and Feta Filo Pie

Makes a 20cm pie approx

500g frozen leaf spinach – defrosted, water squeezed out and roughly chopped

1 large onion – finely chopped

2 garlic cloves

200g block feta cheese – crumbled into chunks

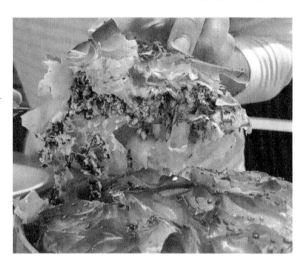

4 tbsp toasted pine nuts

3 eggs

Drizzle of olive oil

Salt and pepper to taste

1 x 450g box filo pastry

125g melted butter

3 tbsp olive oil

1. Pre heat the oven to 200C/400F/gas6
2. Heat the oil in a heavy based pan and fry the onion gently until softened. Add the garlic, fry for a few more minutes, then remove from the heat and allow to cool.
3. Mix the spinach with the onions, pine nuts and feta cheese. Taste and add salt and pepper if necessary. Add the eggs and stir everything together.
4. Mix the melted butter and olive oil together, unfold the filo pastry and cut the sheets in half width wise.

5. Brush each sheet with the butter/oil mixture, overlapping the sheets and draping a good amount of pastry over the edge of the dish. Aim to have approx 3 sheets deep over the surface and sides of the dish.

6. Pile the spinach filling in to the dish and level, finish with a sheet of filo pastry over the top, then fold the pastry edges up and crinkle them around the edge of the dish. Use another buttered sheet of pastry to crinkle over the centre of the pie. Brush over the top of the pie with more melted butter and bake the pie for about 45 minutes. The pastry should be a good golden colour, if it begins to look too dark, turn the oven down to 180C/350F/Gas4.

7. This pie is best served warm.

Use as much of the pastry as you need to, you may not need to use it all.

Spinach & Tomato Lasagne

Serves 6 – 8

This is an old favourite, I have lightened the recipe by using cornflour to thicken the sauce and using only a little cheese.

Tomato sauce

1 large onion, finely chopped

3 medium carrots, finely diced

2 sticks celery, finely diced

1 tbsp oil

1 large red pepper, finely diced

1 clove garlic, finely chopped

1 tin chopped tomatoes

3 tbsp tomato puree

½ tsp dried mixed herbs

1 tsp soft brown sugar

Salt & pepper to taste

Spinach sauce

8 blocks frozen spinach, defrosted

500ml milk

3 heaped tbsp cornflour

3 cloves

2 bay leaves

1 tsp grated nutmeg

Salt & pepper to taste

50g mature cheddar cheese, grated

Approx. 9 sheets lasagne

1. Make the tomato sauce: heat the oil in a heavy based pan. Add the finely chopped onion, carrot, celery pepper and garlic. Fry for a few minutes.
2. Add the tinned tomatoes, tomato puree, mixed herbs and soft brown sugar. Stir to combine, bring to a simmer. Put a lid on the pan and turn the heat down low. Simmer for 20mins.
3. Make the spinach sauce: Pour the milk into a heavy based pan, add the cloves, bay leaves & grated nutmeg, heat gently until the milk is a simmering point. Remove the cloves & bay leaves.
4. Add enough water to the cornflour to make a paste the consistency of cream. Add it slowly to the hot milk, stirring continuously until the sauce thickens and boils for a few seconds. Remove from the heat.
5. Chop the spinach and add to the sauce. Season with salt & pepper to taste.
6. Pre heat the oven to 190C/375F/Gas5
7. Layer up the lasagne by spooning a layer of tomato sauce into the bottom of an oven proof dish approx. 24 x 19cm. Cover with a lasagne sheets. Add a layer of spinach sauce & a layer of tomato sauce & more lasagne. Repeat again to finish the tomato sauce, cover with lasagne, then finish with the remaining spinach sauce. Sprinkle over the cheese.

8. Bake in the oven for 45 mins or until the lasagne is hot, bubbling and browned on top. Once ready, remove from the oven and allow to sit for 10 mins before serving.

Hints, Tips and Variations

Freezable, re heat in a microwave.

For dairy free, use plant based milk & lactose free cheese.

Vary the vegetables in the sauce, try courgette, squash, celeriac…

Spicy Pomelo Salad

Pomelo has a similar, slightly more perfumed flavour to grapefruit, it's a large fruit, available over Christmas and into new year. The pith and skin between the segments is tough and strong. Peel it all away to leave the segmented flesh.

Serves 2

½ pomelo

2 tbsp vegetable oil

1 small onion, finely sliced

1 fat clove garlic, finely sliced

1 medium sized red chilli, deseeded & finely chopped

1 spring onion, finely sliced

2 tbsp cashew nuts, toasted & chopped

1 tbsp lime juice

2 tsp light soya sauce

2 tsp sugar

Small handful fresh coriander, chopped

1. Peel & segment the pomelo, remove the membranes around the segments, then break the segments into bite size pieces. Put them into a large bowl.
2. Heat the oil in a frying pan or wok. Toast the cashew nuts until golden, remove from the pan, drain on kitchen paper and roughly chop. Add the

sliced onion & garlic to the pan, fry until golden brown. Remove from the pan & drain on kitchen paper.

3. Add the browned onion & garlic, chopped cashew nuts, sliced chilli & spring onion to the pomelo. Mix together gently.

4. Mix the lime juice, soya sauce & sugar together, pour over the pomelo and garnish with coriander.

Aubergine, Peppers & Tomatoes

These three are really fruits as they grow from the flower of their parent plant and carry seeds. All are members of the nightshade family along with potatoes and can be joint irritants in arthritis sufferers.

Nutrients include niacin, potassium, vitamins A and C, as well as some B vitamins.

Aubergine

One of the most beautiful fruits of the edible plant world it comes in a range of sizes and colours, the most common being a dark purple form with glossy skin.

Aubergine is not particularly nice raw and is usually baked, roasted or fried, before being made into a dish. The flesh is a mild flavour and acts like a sponge, soaking up any oil or juices. It's popular in Mediterranean and Middle Eastern cuisine and works well as a dip or casserole, mixed with other vegetables and flavours.

Older recipes call for aubergine to be salted to remove bitter juices, modern varieties really don't need this as the bitterness has been bred out of the plant. Look for firm, glossy specimens without soft or wrinkled patches.

Peppers

These include sweet bell peppers and chillies.

Peppers and chillies start off green on the plant and progress through yellow and orange to red as they ripen.

Another nightshade plant, some people find that the pepper skin is hard to digest. The easiest way to do this is by charring the pepper over a gas flame or roasting under the grill, sealing it into a plastic bag and scrapping the skin off once the pepper is cold. Charring like this improves the flavour and texture of pepper flesh. However if you want to stuff and bake your pepper, keep the skin on as it helps the pepper stay in shape.

The seeds and pith of chillies are one of the hottest parts with capsaicin causing the heat in chillies. Its medicinal qualities include blood cleansing, stimulation of circulation and a digestive aid.

Tomatoes

Tomatoes are the mainstay of many diets across the world. There is nothing nicer, if you are growing your own, to be able to pick and eat a ripe tomato straight off the vine.

From salads to sauces, casseroles and ketchup, the way to tell if a tomato is going to taste good is to pick it up and smell it. If it has that strong tomato vine smell it should taste good too.

Tomatoes are a major source of lycopene, an antioxidant that gets stronger the longer tomatoes are cooked. Tomatoes are also a good source of potassium, folate, vitamins C & K. Try to store tomatoes out of the fridge for the best taste and texture.

Summer Roast Aubergine & Feta Cheese Salad

Serves 4

I always find aubergine a challenge, my kids are not particularly keen. This got the thumbs up though!

1 large aubergine

2 tbsp oil

½ bulb fennel, finely sliced

200g pack feta cheese

3 tbsp chives, finely chopped

1 tbsp mint leaves, finely shredded

16 cherry tomatoes, halved

Rind and juice of 1 lemon

2 tbsp good olive oil

1. Heat the oven to 200C/400F/Gas6.
2. Cut the aubergine into 1cm cubes, put into a roasting tin, season with salt & pepper, drizzle with 2 tablespoons of oil, toss well and roast for 20 - 30 mins, until well browned around the edges, turning half way through.
3. Crumble the feta cheese into a large salad bowl, add the finely sliced fennel, including any fronds, halved tomatoes, chives, mint, and lemon rind. Toss everything together well and add the lemon juice and olive oil.
4. Remove the aubergine from the oven, add hot to the salad, tossing well and serve.

Hints, Tips and Adaptations

Gluten free, vegetarian

Use courgette instead of aubergine

Try thinly sliced celery instead of fennel

Ricotta, Walnut & Herb Aubergine Rolls

Serves 2

These are great, eat them hot or cold.

1 medium aubergine

2 tbsps. olive oil

100g ricotta cheese

20g walnuts

1 tbsp. parsley, chopped

1 tbsp. chives, chopped

20g sundried tomatoes, drained & chopped

1 tsp. balsamic vinegar

¼ tsp. ras en hanout spice blend

Small clove garlic, chopped

Salt & pepper

Wooden bamboo skewer, soaked in water for a few mins.

1 tbsp. yogurt

1 tbsp. tahini paste

1-2 tbsps. water

1. Heat the grill to a high heat, slice the aubergine into 5mm slices, you should get 6 and brush each side with a little oil. Put onto a baking sheet

and grill on both sides until golden brown. Remove and cool on kitchen paper.

2. Heat the oven to 200c/400F/Gas6.

3. Mix the chopped sundried tomatoes, walnuts, parsley, chives, balsamic vinegar, garlic & ras en hanout together. Season to taste, divide between the aubergine slices and spread over them in an even layer.

4. Roll each slice up and thread onto the skewer to keep everything together. Either eat the rolls as they are or place back on the baking sheet and bake in the oven for 10 mins.

5. Mix the yogurt, tahini and enough water to make a creamy, drizzly dressing.

6. Serve on a bed of salad with the dressing drizzled over the top.

Hints, Tips and Adaptations

Gluten free, vegetarian

Use a large courgette

Swap the walnuts for hazelnuts, pistachios, pecans or almonds or omit if you're allergic.

Omit the tahini if you're allergic or don't like it. Add a few drops of Maggie seasoning to taste or a little Dijon Dressing.

Baked Eggs en Poivron

Serves 1

Use a large pepper here to ensure enough room for the egg.

½ red, orange or yellow pepper (100g)

1 large egg

30g kale – coarse stalks removed

Small clove garlic

½ tsp ground cumin

½ tsp ground coriander

7g finely grated strong cheese

1 tsp breadcrumbs

½ tsp chopped parsley

½ tsp oil

1. Mix the cheese, crumbs and parsley together.
2. Set the oven to 200C/400F/Gas6
3. Remove the core, pith & seeds from the pepper half, leaving the stalk intact.
4. Put the pepper half on a baking sheet and roast for 10min.
5. Heat ½ tsp oil in a small pan over a medium heat. Cook the onion & garlic for a few minutes until soft.
6. Add the ground spices, cook for a few seconds, then add the kale and a splash of water. Place the lid on the pan, reduce the heat to low and cook for 1 min to soften the kale.

7. Remove the pan from the heat, season the kale with salt & pepper then pack round the inside of the pepper while still hot, ensuring there is enough room for the egg.

8. Crack the egg into the pepper, sprinkle with the cheesy crumbs and bake for 15min. This will give you a runny egg yolk, if you like your eggs more cooked, give it another 5 minutes or so in the oven.

Basic Tomato Sauce

Makes about 600ml

1 large onion

2 cloves garlic – squashed & the skins removed

2 x 400g tins of tomatoes or about 1 Kg of really ripe, fresh tomatoes

Bunch of herbs – rosemary, thyme, bay leaf, parsley (optional)

Drizzle of oil

Salt, pepper and soft brown sugar to taste

1. Chop the onion & sautee with a drizzle of oil to soften and colour slightly. Add the garlic and tomatoes, bring to a simmer with the bunch of herbs and cook for about 20min until the sauce has thickened slightly.
2. Remove the herbs, blitz with a blender and adjust seasoning, if there is a bitter edge, add a little sugar.

If using fresh tomatoes, there is no need to skin them unless the skins are either very thick. If you want a smooth sauce, pass the sauce through a sieve or mooli once blitzed to remove seeds and skins.

More fresh herbs can be added to the sauce at the last minute to change flavours slightly – basil, parsley, thyme, rosemary etc.

Chermoula Aubergine with Couscous

Makes 2

1 garlic clove

1 tsp. ground cinnamon

1 tsp. ground coriander

1 small red chilli

½ tsp. paprika

¼ preserved lemon

2 tbsps. olive oil

1 medium aubergine

75g couscous

½ tsp. vegetable stock powder

small handful sultanas

1 tbsp. chopped coriander

1 tsp. chopped mint

2 tbsps. toasted, flaked almonds

2 spring onions, finely sliced

1 small tomato, de seeded and chopped

squeeze of lemon juice

1. Preheat the oven to 200C/gas 6

2. Make the chermoula, mix the garlic, cumin, coriander, chilli, paprika, preserved lemon and enough oil to moisten the mixture to a sloppy paste.

3. Cut the aubergine in half length wise and score deep diagonal criss cross scores in the cut side, being careful not to cut the skin.

4. Spoon over the chermoula and rub into the cuts.

5. Place the aubergine on a baking sheet cut side up and roast for about 40 min or until completely soft.

6. Make the couscous – put 75ml water into a small pan, add the vegetable stock powder and sultanas, bring to the boil. Once boiling, pour in the couscous, stir, turn off the heat and place the lid on the pot. Allow to sit while you mix the herbs, almonds, tomato and spring onions together.

7. Remove the lid from the couscous, drizzle over the remaining oil and fluff up with a fork. Mix with the herb mixture, check for seasoning and serve warm, piled on top of the aubergine halves.

Grilled Ras en Hanout Aubergine with Quinoa Salad

Serves 2

This is a great way to eat aubergine. Soft, but full of flavour with a tasty quinoa salad. Ras en hanout is a Middle Eastern spice mix.

1 med aubergine

2 tsps. ras en hanout

1 tbsp. olive oil

70g quinoa

70ml water

½ tsp. vegetable bouillon

10cm piece cucumber, cubed

12 cherry tomatoes, quartered

16 black olives

Small handful coriander or parsley, chopped

¼ of a bulb of fennel, thinly sliced

1. Pre heat the grill to high heat, use the middle grilling level.
2. Rub the aubergine pieces with the oil and sprinkle over the ras en hanout, pressing it into the aubergine to make it stick. Put the aubergine onto a baking sheet and under the grill, turning to brown it on all sides. Remove from the grill and allow to cool for 5 minutes.

3. Put the water, quinoa and vegetable bouillon into a pan with a lid. Bring to the boil and simmer for 10 mins to cook. Allow to sit for 10 mins to absorb any excess moisture.

4. Stir through the cucumber, cherry tomatoes, olives and fennel and herbs. Taste and season with salt & pepper if necessary, divide between 2 bowls.

5. Serve each bowl topped with 2 quarters of the warm aubergine.

Hints, Tips and Adaptations

Gluten free, dairy free, vegetarian & vegan

Use couscous instead of quinoa

If you don't have ras en hanout or find it too pungent, use salt & pepper

Change the herbs and vegetables for a different flavour.

Roast Tomato Soup

Serves 6

400g ripe tomatoes

1 tin plum tomatoes

2 onions

1 tin coconut milk

1 tbsp. soft brown sugar

Small bunch coriander

1 garlic clove

2cm piece of ginger – grated

1 med red chilli

1. Heat the oven to 200C/400F/gas 6. Cut the tomatoes in half, cut the onion into wedges, drizzle with olive oil, season and roast for about 30 minutes until starting to brown round the edges. Remove from the oven, once cool enough to handle pinch away the tomato skins.
2. In a large pan, drizzle a little olive oil and cook the ginger, chilli and coriander for a few minutes. Add the tinned tomatoes and coconut milk. Simmer for a few minutes with the lid on, then turn off the heat and allow to sit until the tomatoes and onions are ready.
3. Add the roast tomatoes and onions, sugar and fish sauce. Bring to the boil, simmer for 10 min, check seasoning, blend and serve.

Roasted Vegetables with Red Pepper Sauce

Serves 2

Give your vegetables a lift with this sauce which reduces and flavours the vegetables as it cooks.

160g squash, cut into cubes or slices

230g cauliflower, cut into large florets

160g broccoli, cut into large florets

1 small onion, cut into wedges

1 red pepper

20ml oil

2 cloves garlic

½ tsp. chilli flakes

½ tsp. smoked paprika

Salt & pepper

1. Heat the oven to 200C/400F/Gas6.
2. Puree the red pepper, garlic and oil together in a food processor or blender.
3. Mix well with the vegetables, sprinkle over the smoked paprika, chilli flakes, salt & pepper.
4. Bake for 30mins, stirring everything round after 15 mins. The vegetables should be tender with crispy, browned edges.

Hints Tips & Adaptations

Gluten free, dairy free, vegetarian, vegan

Re-heat in a microwave

Try sweet potatoes, new potatoes, green beans etc as alternatives

Add beans, chick peas or firm tofu as a protein element.

A great dish on it's own or as an accompaniment

Scrambled Egg Shakshuka

Serves 4

My children are not great egg eaters. They will however eat scrambled eggs quite happily. Shakshuka is normally made by poaching the eggs in the sauce. It works equally well with scrambled.

4 to 8 eggs, depending on whether you have big eaters or not.

½ tsp. caraway seeds

1 tbsp olive oil + extra for drizzling

1 medium onion, thinly sliced

1 red pepper, thinly sliced

Pinch of chilli flakes, or to taste

½ tsp. ground cumin

½ tsp. sweet smoked paprika

1 large ripe tomato, chopped

1 tin cherry tomatoes in juice

50g feta cheese

2 tbsps. coriander leaves

1. Heat 1 tbsp olive oil in a heavy based frying pan. Fry the caraway seeds for a few seconds, then add the sliced onion and pepper. Fry for a few minutes to soften and start to colour.

2. Add the ground cumin, smoked paprika & chilli flakes. Stir and add the chopped tomato. Cook for 2 minutes, then add the tinned cherry tomatoes.

3. Simmer gently for 20 minutes without a lid to allow the juices to reduce and the flavour to intensify.

4. Heat the oven to 200C/400F/Gas6

5. One at a time, beat each egg with a little salt & pepper, make a dip in the tomato mixture and fill with the scrambled egg.

6. Once all the eggs are in the pan, crumble over the feta cheese and put the pan into the oven. Cook for 10mins.

7. Remove from the oven, sprinkle over the coriander and serve.

Hints, Tips and Variations

Gluten free, vegetarian, dairy free if you omit the feta cheese.

Swap the caraway seed for cumin seed.

Use parsley instead of coriander

Bake whole eggs in the mixture instead of scrambling.

Spinach and Red Pepper Roulade

Serves 4

6 eggs separated

300g frozen leaf spinach – de frosted, water squeezed out and finely chopped

Salt, pepper and nutmeg

Filling

Drizzle of olive oil

1 small red onion – finely chopped

2 large red peppers – deseeded and chopped

1 tsp paprika

1 clove garlic – chopped

½ tin chopped tomatoes

Salt and pepper to taste.

1. Line a Swiss roll tin with a double layer of non-stick baking paper. Allowing the edges of the paper to stick up above the sides of the tin.
2. Make the filling. Heat the olive oil in a saucepan and gently cook the onion until soft. Add the garlic, paprika, red pepper and cook until softened. Add the tomatoes and simmer until most of the juice has evaporated. Set aside
3. Preheat the oven to 190C/375F/gas5.
4. Stir the egg yolks, salt, pepper and nutmeg into the spinach.

5. Whip the egg whites to stiff peak and fold into the spinach. Pour the mixture into the prepared baking sheet and spread level. Bake in the oven for 10 – 12 min.

6. Put a clean tea towel onto your surface with a piece of greaseproof paper covering it. Remove the roulade from the oven, flip it onto the greaseproof paper and remove the original non-stick baking parchment.

7. Spread the red pepper mixture over the roulade, leaving a 2cm gap around the edges.

8. Using the greaseproof paper, roll up from the long edge closest to you, place onto a warmed serving dish and slice to serve.

Tomato Risotto

Serves 4

This is a great risotto, full of flavour and texture. As with my other risottos, once it's simmering, put a lid on the pan and let it simmer. Using a mug to measure cuts out any need for scales.

1 mugful (230g) risotto rice

1 small leek, sliced

1 medium carrot, diced

1 stick celery, diced

1 tbsp oil

1 clove garlic, finely sliced

2 spring onions

6 pieces sundried tomato, roughly chopped

1 tin chopped tomatoes + 1 tin of water

½ mug white wine

1 tsp chicken or vegetable stock powder

¼ tsp ground turmeric

2 spring onions, finely sliced

Parmesan cheese

Parsley

Pinch of sugar

1. Heat the oil in a heavy based pan, add the sliced leek, diced carrot & celery. Fry gently to soften for a few minutes, then add the garlic.
2. Add the rice and stir well. Cook for a couple of minutes, stirring from time to time, then add the wine. The pan will be quite hot and it will bubble.
3. Add the pieces of sundried tomato, turmeric & stock powder then stir in the tinned tomatoes plus one tin of water. Stir well, bring to a simmer, put a lid on the pan and cook gently for 15 - 20 minutes. Stirring from time to time.
4. Taste and adjust the seasoning & texture, adding the pinch of sugar if necessary and extra water if the risotto is too dry for your liking. Stir through the spring onions, pile into bowls, sprinkle over Parmesan cheese and chopped parsley.

Hints, Tips and Adaptations

Vegetarian if using veg stock, vegan if you omit the cheese or swap for a vegan alternative.

Re-heat in a microwave.

Swap celery for fennel. Use tinned tomatoes with extra herbs/chilli/garlic for flavour.

Potatoes

Probably the most universal and highly consumed vegetable belonging to the nightshade family. Potatoes are rich in nutrients, particularly potassium and reasonable amounts of B and C vitamins, magnesium, manganese, iron and zinc. They are reasonably low in calories and are made up of approximately two thirds starchy carbohydrate and 10 percent protein.

They can be baked, boiled, steamed, fried, roasted, mashed, used to thicken soups & casseroles.

There's nothing nicer than a fluffy baked potato with a crispy skin, boiled waxy new potatoes drizzled with butter or a creamy mash flavoured with nutmeg.

What to look for

There are literally hundreds of varieties of potato, with a whole range of shapes, sizes and cooking qualities. Some are good bakers, others are good chippers. Some are waxy, some are floury.

Potatoes normally have white or slightly creamy yellow flesh, some have white skins, others pink or red, there are even a few blue potatoes. Only a few varieties are available to buy commercially. It's down to personal taste whether you prefer a floury or waxy potato, but it's amazing when you start to taste the different varieties, how diverse they are in flavour and texture.

When you're looking at potatoes, look at the skins, they should be a little bit damp with minimal bruising or blemishes, no sprouts or green patches.

Sweet potatoes

These are starchy, sweet tasting vegetables belonging to the bindweed family. They can have pink or white flesh and are a good source of fibre, beta carotene, B vitamins, vitamin C, iron, calcium and selenium.

They tend to give a wetter result than ordinary potatoes when baked, chipped or mashed, but make a delicious curry and creamy soup.

Roast Potatoes

Floury potatoes: e.g. King Edward, Desiree, Rooster, Cara.

Allow around 225g/8oz per person. This gives about 3 each

Cooking oil to fill the bottom of a roasting tin by about 5mm

1. Pre heat the oven to 200C/Gas6.
2. Par boil the potatoes in salted water for 10 min. Drain, hold the lid of the pan in place firmly and give the pan a good shake to roughen the edges of the potato.
3. Heat the oil in the roasting tin, carefully tip in the potatoes and baste and turn them to coat them in the oil.
4. Put back into the oven and roast for 30 – 40 min, turning about half way through.
5. Before serving, drain well and if necessary keep in a warm oven uncovered and not piled up.

Hasselback Potatoes

Baking potatoes

Rosemary leaves

Olive oil

Salt & pepper

1. Pre heat the oven to 200C/Gas6
2. Use a chopstick or wooden spoon handle either side of the potato and cut slices approx. a half centimetre thick across the potatoes. The chopsticks will stop you cutting all the way through.
3. Push the rosemary sprigs down into the potato slices to separate them. Drizzle with a little oil and season with salt & pepper.
4. Roast in the oven for about an hour until they're golden brown and crisp.

Roast Seasoned Vegetables

Use Potatoes, sweet potatoes, parsnips, carrots, beetroot or courgettes

Drizzle of oil

1 – 2 tsp vegetable bouillon powder.

Black pepper

1. Heat the oven to 200C/Gas 6
2. Cut the potatoes or other vegetables into wedges or sticks. Put into a large bowl drizzle with oil and sprinkle with vegetable powder and black pepper.
3. Use your hands to mix everything together well, transfer to a baking sheet and roast for between 30 and 45 minutes, turning once or twice. It will depend how thick your potato or vegetable pieces are and the mixture you use.

Sweet Potato & Ginger Soup

Serves about 6

1 large onion

1 tbsp oil

3 medium sweet potatoes

1 can coconut milk

1 small clove garlic, peeled and left whole

Thumb sized piece of root ginger, finely grated

1 red chilli, deseeded & chopped

Vegetable or chicken stock

Juice of ½ lime

Salt & pepper

1. Peel and roughly chop the onion, heat the oil in a heavy based pan and fry the onion gently to soften and colour slightly.
2. Peel the sweet potatoes, cut into chunks and add to the onion along with the garlic, ginger and chilli. Fry for a few minutes longer, then add the coconut milk and enough stock to just cover the vegetables. Bring to the boil, put the lid on the pan and simmer for 20mins.
3. Blend the soup with a hand blender or similar, add more stock if the soup is too thick. Adjust the seasoning and add the lime juice. The soup is now ready to serve.

Sweet Potato & Red Pepper Chilli

Serves 4

This is great, quick and easy to make, spice it up or down or miss the chilli out completely if you're not a fan.

4 small sweet potatoes, peeled & cut into chunks

1 red pepper – de seeded & cut into chunks

1 onion - sliced

1 red chilli – optional

1 large clove garlic - sliced

2cm piece of root ginger – grated or shredded

1 can red kidney beans – drained & rinsed

1 can coconut milk

100g fresh spinach

1 tsp ground cumin

1 tsp ground coriander

1 tbsp oil

1. Fry the onion, pepper and sweet potato for a few minutes to soften the onion and add a bit of colour to the sweet potato.

2. Add the chilli, ginger, garlic, cumin and coriander. Stir in and add the kidney beans and coconut milk.
3. Bring to a simmer and cook until the sweet potato is tender (5 to 10mins).
4. Stir through the spinach and adjust the seasoning.

Hints, Tips and Adaptations

Dairy free, gluten free, freezable, microwavable.

Use double cream if you don't like coconut milk

Add in other firm vegetables for a change eg squash, carrots, mushrooms, aubergines, courgettes etc.

Change the beans to chickpeas, other beans or brown lentils

Warm Salad of Sweet Potato, Quinoa and Lentils

Serves 4

This is a delicious dish, full of protein from the quinoa and lentils. It doesn't feel like salad as it's served warm.

800g sweet potatoes, peeled and cut into 2cm cubes

150g quinoa

150g green lentils

1. Heat the oven to 200C/400F/Gas6.
2. Spread out the sweet potato on a baking sheet, sprinkle with salt & pepper, drizzle with oil and roast for 20 mins.
3. Measure the lentils into a mug, tip into a pan and cook with an equal quantity of vegetable stock for 20 mins. Drain any excess liquid away.
4. Measure the quinoa into a mug, tip into a pan and cook with an equal quantity of vegetable stock for 10 mins. Allow to sit and absorb any excess liquid.

½ red onion finely chopped

Seeds of 1 pomegranate

2 tbsps. preserved lemon, finely diced

3 tbsps. olive or rapeseed oil

Juice of ½ lemon

Large handful of herbs, I used parsley, tarragon and mint, chopped

4 handfuls spicy salad leaves, I used watercress (optional).

1. Mix the chopped red onion, pomegranate seeds, preserved lemon, oil, lemon juice and herbs together.
2. Add the warm lentils, quinoa and sweet potato, toss together well and serve while still warm either as it is on a bed of spicy leaves.

Hints, Tips and Adaptations

Dairy free, gluten free, vegetarian, suitable for vegans.

Use potatoes, squash, carrots or other root vegetables etc instead of sweet potato.

If you can't find preserved lemons, use the rind of 1 lemon.

Try orange segments instead of pomegranate seeds.

GIFT CERTIFICATE

WE'RE PLEASED TO GIVE YOU

£25

OFF A CUSTOM IN PERSON OR
ONLINE 1 TO 1 CLASS

Voucher code: VB25

TERMS & CONDITIONS

1. This gift certificate is not redeemable for cash.

2. This gift certificate is non-transferable and resale
is prohibited.

3. If a gift certificate is lost, stolen, destroyed or used
without permission, a replacement will not be provided in
these circumstances.

4. This gift certificate is not to be combined with other
vouchers and is not valid with other promos and offers.

5. To redeem this voucher, choose either a Custom In
Person or Online class at www.Coursesforcooks.com.
Contact us for availability & booking.

WWW.COURSESFORCOOKS.COM

Printed in Great Britain
by Amazon

69134908R00120